MY POCKET
CHAKRA HEALING

MY POCKET
CHAKRA
HEALING

ANYTIME EXERCISES
TO UNBLOCK, BALANCE,
AND STRENGTHEN
YOUR CHAKRAS

HEIDI E. SPEAR

ADAMS MEDIA
NEW YORK LONDON TORONTO SYDNEY NEW DELHI

Δadamsmedia

Adams Media
An Imprint of Simon & Schuster, Inc.
100 Technology Center Drive
Stoughton, MA 02072

First Adams Media trade paperback edition September 2019

ADAMS MEDIA and colophon are trademarks of Simon & Schuster.

For information about special discounts for bulk purchases, please contact Simon & Schuster Special Sales at 1-866-506-1949 or business@simonandschuster.com.

The Simon & Schuster Speakers Bureau can bring authors to your live event. For more information or to book an event contact the Simon & Schuster Speakers Bureau at 1-866-248-3049 or visit our website at www.simonspeakers.com.

Interior images by Eric Andrews

Manufactured in China

10 9 8 7 6 5 4 3

Library of Congress Cataloging-in-Publication Data
Names: Spear, Heidi E., author.
Title: My pocket chakra healing / Heidi E. Spear.
Series: My pocket.
Description: Avon, Massachusetts: Adams Media, 2019.
Identifiers: LCCN 2019015831 | ISBN 9781507211199 (pb) | ISBN 9781507211205 (ebook)
Subjects: LCSH: Chakra (Hinduism) | Healing--Religious aspects--Hinduism.
Classification: LCC BL1215.C45 S642 2019 | DDC 131--dc23
LC record available at https://lccn.loc.gov/2019015831

ISBN 978-1-5072-1119-9
ISBN 978-1-5072-1120-5 (ebook)

Contains material adapted from the following title published by Adams Media, an Imprint of Simon & Schuster, Inc.: *The Everything® Guide to Chakra Healing* by Heidi E. Spear, copyright © 2011, ISBN 978-1-4405-2584-1.

CONTENTS

INTRODUCTION

Are you looking for an easy way to practice self-care while connecting your mind, body, and spirit? If so, chakra healing could be the answer. The chakras are seven bright, glowing energy centers that control the flow of life-force energy within your body. Sometimes the chakras spin too slowly, sometimes too quickly, and sometimes just right. If they are spinning just right, energy travels freely to your physical, mental, and energetic bodies. This means you feel healthy, balanced, and happy.

At times, however, your chakras are out of balance. This book will help you learn to recognize when that happens and find balance through a variety of easy-to-follow methods. The experience of chakra healing is creative, magical, surprising, restorative, and cleansing. Chakra healing improves your mind, body, and spirit so you become more connected with wisdom, happiness, and the energy of love and gratitude that ties you to the universe.

In *My Pocket Chakra Healing*, you'll learn what exactly chakras are, the correlation between your chakras and various body parts, and how chakra healing goes hand-in-hand with modern medicine and any spiritual choices you make. You'll also find more than fifty exercises you can do at home, at work, or on the go to bring awareness and balance to your chakras, including how to:

* Use crystals to connect with specific chakras
* Practice yoga poses that bring awareness to your chakras
* Meditate to focus on your chakras
* Heal energetic disturbances with aromatherapy sessions
* Manifest your desires by balancing your chakras

As you delve into these exercises, you'll notice that some of them will make you feel good right away, but others will require regular and sustained practice to reap the benefits. Don't give up if an exercise doesn't pay off right away—keep at it, and eventually you will see results! You can also jump around to the sections that look interesting to you, and go from there. Enjoy the process and feel free to personalize the ideas to match your lifestyle, energy profile, and preferences.

As you read this book, remember that you are unique. Go at your own pace and make a commitment to honor and listen to yourself as you explore your chakras. Follow your intuition and it will lead you to a life full of peace, joy, and love.

PART 1

THE BASICS
OF CHAKRAS

CHAPTER 1

WHAT ARE CHAKRAS?

Chakras are spinning energy centers that directly influence your well-being and how consciously and happily you create your life's path. When all of the chakras are balanced, you feel safe, creative, strong, and secure in yourself and in relationships. You are comfortable speaking your mind, and your thoughts come together with clarity and ease. You also feel connected to your intuition and the vital energy of the universe. Chakras can sometimes become imbalanced—but fortunately there are ways to bring your deficient or excessive chakras into balance. This chapter presents the basics of chakra theory and introduces the seven major chakras of the body.

YOUR RENEWABLE ENERGY CENTERS

Chakra is Sanskrit for "wheel or disc," and the chakras are vortices of energy that spin as glowing wheels of light inside you. There are seven major chakras in the body. Throughout your life, what you experience on the outside (your environment, friends, and family) as well as what you experience inwardly (your thoughts and emotions) will affect your chakras and consequently your body and mind. When the chakras are all spinning in balance, you will find it easier to be doing the things in your life that you want to do, with ease and joy. You will also be able to tap into your true desires and create the life that you truly want to live.

Each of the chakras can be overactive or deficient, however, which means they are blocked and not in balance. Chakras can be out of balance since your time in the womb, or even earlier: in the yogic view, the karma you carry from your past lives is stored in the chakras. By becoming familiar with the physical and psychological signs and symptoms related to the functions of each chakra, you begin to understand how the chakras affect your mental, physical, and spiritual health. Then you will know where to focus your healing energy.

Each chakra's root is planted in the major current of energy that runs up and down the center of the spinal column. This line of energy is called the *sushumna* nadi. In between each of the chakras, along the sushumna, two other major currents of energy (*nadis*), cross back and forth. These are called the *ida* and *pingala* nadis. From the third eye, the ida curves to the left first, in a semicircular shape, to cross the sushumna at the Throat Chakra. Then it curves in a semicircle to the right before crossing the sushumna and pingala at the Heart Chakra. The pingala nadi curves down the right side of the body first, from the third eye, and mirrors the pattern of the ida.

There are different estimations of where the nadis meet with each crisscross. One view is that the nadis cross in between the chakras, and those currents cause the chakras to spin, while the other view states that the ida and pingala cross at each chakra. Either way, the relevant point is that the chakras are affected by the flow of energy as it travels along the sushumna, ida, and pingala nadis.

A BRIDGE FROM NOW TO ETERNITY

The chakras are the bridge along which you can guide your awareness, up and down, to move the life-force energy of the earth and of the eternal oneness that connects all energy and all beings. The energy of the earth that rises up from your Root Chakra is called *Shakti,* and the energy of pure consciousness that comes down through your Crown Chakra is called *Shiva*. As you work with the chakras, the goal is to unite Shiva and Shakti (life force and eternal consciousness). Shakti energy in the Tantric view is called *Kundalini*—the same energy with another name. Visualizing where each chakra is located is an important part of how you will tap into their energies and correct imbalances.

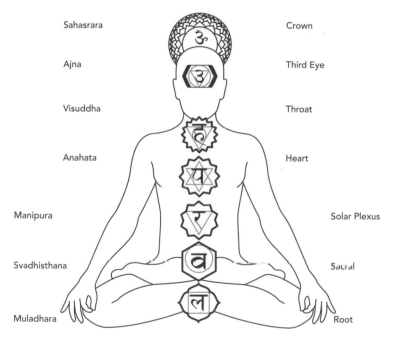

Sahasrara	Crown
Ajna	Third Eye
Visuddha	Throat
Anahata	Heart
Manipura	Solar Plexus
Svadhisthana	Sacral
Muladhara	Root

The seven major chakras in the body.

As you learn about the chakras and practice visualizing them, it will become second nature. Your relationship to your chakras will continue to deepen.

FIRST: THE ROOT CHAKRA (MULADHARA)

The first chakra is called the Root Chakra, *Muladhara* in Sanskrit. The Root Chakra hooks into the base of the spine, in the area called the perineum. This is the area between the genitals and the anus. The Root Chakra's energy connects right to the earth's energy. You can draw energy upward to revitalize you, or send energy downward to ground yourself. To visualize where the Root Chakra is, take a deep nourishing breath in through the nose, and imagine the breath traveling down into the perineum. While your attention is there, imagine a red glow energizing that area. Exhale through your nostrils and imagine any negative energy flowing out with the breath. Repeat this a few times.

Kundalini Energy

It is said that the life-force energy of Kundalini lies coiled as a serpent goddess at the base of the spine, wrapped three-and-a-half times around the Root Chakra. As you awaken the Root Chakra, Kundalini energy rises up to unite with Shiva energy and transfers energy to each chakra on its way up to the Crown Chakra.

SECOND: THE SACRAL CHAKRA (SVADHISTHANA)

To visualize the location of the second chakra, *Svadhisthana*, turn your attention to your lower abdomen, below the navel. The root of the second chakra is said to be located in the first lumbar vertebra of the spine. *Svadhisthana* (also called the Sacral Chakra) is usually translated as "sweetness" (*svad*) or "one's own place" (*sva*). This chakra is associated with the pleasures of life: sexuality, creativity, and trust in intimate relationships. To lead your mind to where this chakra is, close your eyes, breathe in deeply through the nose, and expand the belly as you envision the breath flowing into the area below your navel. Hold the breath for a moment, picturing an orange glow while keeping your attention on this area of Svadhisthana energy. Exhale slowly, drawing the belly in, expelling the air as you imagine unwanted negativity leaving the body through your nose. Repeat this a few times.

THIRD: THE SOLAR PLEXUS CHAKRA (MANIPURA)

Manipura is the name of the third chakra, which is located in the solar plexus region of the body. This chakra is said to be rooted in the area of the seventh and eighth thoracic vertebrae. Its name means "lustrous gem," and the chakra is often depicted as glowing yellow. To become familiar with this chakra's location, place your hand on your front body between your navel and sternum. Inhale so that your body expands into that hand, and as you breathe in imagine you're inhaling a warm, yellow ribbon of light. Then exhale, releasing tension from the midsection. Repeat this visualization with breath a few times.

FOURTH: THE HEART CHAKRA (ANAHATA)

The fourth chakra, *Anahata*, means "unstruck." This is the Heart Chakra, located at the center of the chest, at the fourth thoracic vertebra. To visualize the placement of this chakra, use the three-part yogic breath. On the inhale, breathe deeply and expand the belly, and on the same inhale expand the rib cage and then the chest. As you expand the chest, imagine it filling up with a green glow. On the exhale, slowly let the breath go. Repeat this a few times.

FIFTH: THE THROAT CHAKRA (VISUDDHA)

The Visuddha Chakra, or Throat Chakra, is the fifth chakra. *Visuddha* means "purification." This chakra is located just above the collarbone, at the third cervical vertebra. It is the bridge from the Heart Chakra to the third eye. To drop your awareness into the placement of the Throat Chakra, close your eyes and imagine you have just taken a large sip of clear blue water. As the water goes down your throat, it washes over the Throat Chakra. Imagine this for a moment: clear blue water running effortlessly down the throat where the Throat Chakra spins.

SIXTH: THE THIRD EYE CHAKRA (AJNA)

The Third Eye Chakra is sometimes called the Brow Chakra. In Sanskrit, it's *Ajna*, "to perceive." It is located in the space between the eyes and slightly higher than the brow line. To visualize this chakra, gently place the palms of your hands over your eyes, and pivot the hands so that the fingers of the left hand overlap the fingers of the right hand. Place your attention into that space where the hands overlap. Inhale and exhale a few times, imagining indigo-colored energy flowing into that space.

SEVENTH: THE CROWN CHAKRA (SAHASRARA)

Sahasrara, which means "thousandfold," is the name of the seventh chakra, the Crown Chakra. It's located at the top of the head. To visualize this chakra, close your eyes, and allow your breath to come in and out of your body at its own pace. Imagine the glow of any or all of the following colors surrounding the top of your head on all sides: violet, white, and/or gold. Hold your lips in a gentle, easy smile, and continue for a few breaths to allow the glow to envelop your head.

The Metaphor of the Lotus Flower

Sahasrara refers to the image of a lotus flower with one thousand petals. In nature, the lotus flower grows from the mud to blossom beautifully toward the sun. This is a metaphor for the human experience: while you are rooted deeply in the earth and physical body, you can connect to the state of bliss and life-force energy that unites all things.

CHAKRAS PROVIDE A CONNECTION TO NATURE

The basic elements of the living, natural world are interpreted differently in different cultures. In her writing on the chakras, Anodea Judith expands the typical four or five elemental list to seven elements: earth, water, fire, air, sound, light, and thought. Each element corresponds to principles that govern human life in the world, and each corresponds to a particular chakra. Judith's model is an invaluable tool for understanding how you are a mirror of the natural world and how the health of the chakras affects the flow of your life force.

You are not only a mirror of the natural world but also an intricate part of it. Do you often feel cut off from nature when you are in your home, your car, a grocery store, or your workplace? If so, you might be surprised to learn how the elements of the outside world are also within you.

* The Root Chakra is your connection to the earth: supportive, stable, grounding.
* The Sacral Chakra gives you the qualities of water: fluid, flowing, sensual.
* The Solar Plexus Chakra is a billow for your internal fire: transformative heat, self-esteem, will.

* The Heart Chakra is your relationship to air: holds and makes space, connection to others.
* The Throat Chakra supports your sound: self-expression, communication.
* The Third Eye Chakra is your wisdom light: enabling you to see clearly.
* The Crown Chakra opens you up to pure consciousness: unity with all that is.

The elemental correspondences to each chakra are a reminder that you are not separate from the miracles and elements of the natural world. You are as strong, powerful, beautiful, and mysterious as they are.

Knowing that you have all the powerful elements of the universe inside you connects you to the beauty, the wonder, and the ephemeral qualities you see outside. And because of that, for the benefit of your life, the lives of your children, the lives of people you don't even know, and the lives of everything on the planet that provides for you, it's essential to take responsibility for what you put outside. Your chakras need the energy from the sun, moon, water, and vegetation, so find ways by your actions and your intentions to support and honor the earth more.

YOUR BODY AS A PRISM

The healing vital energy of the world can be found everywhere, even in waves of light. Each color of the rainbow vibrates at its own frequency in what you see as white light. A prism refracts the light. If you hold a prism up to natural light, the angles of the prism separate the vibrating waves, and the naked eye sees rainbows coming out of another side.

You can think of the body as working in a similar way. It's as though the universal healing white light gets refracted when it enters the body, and each color sustains a particular chakra. The most widely used modern model of the chakras is to associate them with the colors of the rainbow.

* The Root Chakra responds to the color red.
* The Sacral Chakra responds to the color orange.
* The Solar Plexus Chakra responds to the color yellow.
* The Heart Chakra responds to the color green.
* The Throat Chakra responds to the color blue.
* The Third Eye Chakra responds to the color indigo.
* The Crown Chakra responds to violet, gold, and white.

Blocked chakras tend to balance in response to these colors. At times you might find reports of different colors associated with the chakras. This happens because chakras are energy centers, and ever changing. Some people may have a different experience from others.

TANTRIC CHAKRA MODEL

The first Tantric translation of the colors of the chakras was translated into English by Sir John Woodroffe, who published this and other texts under his pen name, Arthur Avalon. His famous translation of the chakras with extra notes was published in 1919 in *The Serpent Power*. In it, he translates the detailed experience of meditation on the chakras as written by Pūrṇānanda-Svāmī, in 1577. In *Sat-Cakra-Nirupana*, Pūrṇānanda-Svāmī wrote instructions on how to meditate on the chakras, and their symbolism. This type of information was usually only passed on in India orally and secretly from guru to disciple. It was and is considered sacred and holy because the energies of the earth and of consciousness that flow through the body are considered sacred. That Woodroffe could eventually get this material and receive help interpreting it meant that in the early twentieth century these sacred secrets could be revealed to a wider and English-speaking audience. This is one of the major sources for our understanding of chakra theory today.

You can bring much-needed energy to the chakras by choosing a color to meditate on from Pūrṇānanda-Svāmī's detailed descriptions:

* **The Root Chakra:** a lotus with a square yellow center and crimson petals.
* **The Sacral Chakra:** a vermilion-colored lotus with the water element in its white center.
* **The Solar Plexus Chakra:** a lotus the color of a rain cloud with a red fiery triangle in the center.
* **The Heart Chakra:** a lotus the color of a bandhuka flower with a smoky hexagonal mandala in its center.
* **The Throat Chakra:** a ruddy-colored lotus with a center like the spotless moon, white and pure.
* **The Third Eye Chakra:** a lotus that is pure white, like the moon.
* **The Crown Chakra:** a lotus that is white with red filaments; in the center is the golden sun.

The rainbow model (red, orange, yellow, green, blue, indigo, violet/ white/gold) of the chakras and the model that Pūrṇānanda-Svāmī provides are guides to follow from those who have experienced awareness of the energy fields and watched the meditations work.

The strength of the chakras will respond to the energy around you, and you can help by putting yourself in supportive environments. You do this with all your choices: where you place yourself, whom you spend time with, what you think, what you eat, and if you meditate. Because the higher chakras are associated with colors of a higher vibration such as pure white light, spend some time outside by moonlight. The full moon is astonishingly luminous. Just as you spend time enjoying sunlight, spend time enjoying moonlight. Your higher chakras will be nourished by the interaction, and the effect will touch all the chakras.

AURA COLORS

The auric field appears to have seven layers, each corresponding to one of the seven major chakras. Each layer is a three-dimensional oval shape surrounding the body, and they progress concentrically outward. The layer closest to the body appears a vibrant red when the Root Chakra's energy is radiating in a balanced way, the second layer is orange and reflects the health of the Sacral Chakra, and so on, ending with the seventh layer that shows up as the color violet and corresponds to the Crown Chakra. So, the auric field looks like an egg-shaped rainbow enveloping the body, when all the chakras are in balance.

What Is Your Aura?

Chakra activity projects colors into your aura, or auric field. For some, it's easy to see auras in plain sight. Anyone can see auras in a Kirlian photograph, a kind of energy photography. You can have your aura photographed, and on different days or after meditation, you could see a change in the colors of your auric field.

THE ORIGINS OF CHAKRA THEORY: SACRED EASTERN WISDOM

Chakra theory originates in the yogic tradition, where meditation on the chakras is used on the path of liberation. Before yoga practice became widespread in the West, wisdom and training for chakra meditation was passed on only from guru to disciple, as sacred wisdom. The yogis experienced chakras as glowing brightly, connecting each person to the universal energy and to the strength and power of divine gods and goddesses.

The yogis were primarily interested in chakra meditation for liberation, or nirvana. When Westerners learned about the chakras, they became interested in how these energy centers might affect the physical body and the mind. Today, interest in chakra healing continues to grow. People are curious about how they can participate in their own healing, and they want to understand their own compositions.

Attachment and Aversion

A foundation of the yogic philosophy is that human existence includes suffering. People are attached to their desires, and the attachment ultimately causes them to suffer. People try to avoid things that cause pain, and inevitably suffer. This is called "attachment and aversion," two habits that always lead to suffering. Yogis meditate to achieve liberation from suffering.

HOW CHAKRA THEORY EVOLVED

After Sir John Woodroffe made many foundational texts accessible, Charles Webster Leadbeater became a primary figure in the evolution of chakra theory. He is best known for his books *The Inner Life* (1911) and *The Chakras* (1927). Leadbeater was a member of the school of mystical thought known as Theosophy. The Theosophical Society was established in 1875 as a forum for exploring the mysteries of life. The theories Theosophists believe in adapt yogic philosophy and include reincarnation, karma, the power of thought to affect oneself and one's surroundings, and the existence of worlds of experience beyond the physical. Because these are foundations for them, it's no surprise that the mysterious chakras—which link physical and energetic existence—captured their interest.

Leadbeater and Alice Bailey were among the first to assert that chakra placement suggested a relationship between the chakras and the endocrine system (see Chapter 4). It makes sense that they would be interested to see what else they might discover about the body's energy centers, especially because Theosophists believe that human beings can actively participate in intellectual, spiritual, and physical evolution. The interest of Theosophists in the yogic tradition has been catalytic in the popularization of chakra study. This type of popularization runs the risk of succumbing to adaptations that take the sacredness out of the tradition, and yet, that has not happened to chakra theory.

CHAPTER 2

WHAT IS CHAKRA HEALING?

Chakra healing is much more than healing your physical body. By balancing the chakras, you open up to your fullest potential as a physical and energetic being, which means you have the ultimate potential for health, happiness, and creating the life you want to lead. You will experience ease, joy, and unexpected miracles. By reading this book, you have shown that you already know, however deep inside, that it's possible to live a healthier, more fulfilled life, and you are investigating ways to do it. In Part 2 of this book, you'll learn myriad simple ways you can balance chakras, including crystal and color therapy, meditation, aromatherapy, and yoga and breathing exercises. First, you need a full understanding of how chakra balance leads to overall well-being.

HEALING ON ALL LEVELS

According to chakra theory, when all the chakras are balanced, your body, mind, intuition, and the part of you that is eternal (soul, spirit, source energy, etc.) all work together. At these times, each chakra is functioning well: you sense the state of your body; you express your creative ideas; you have energy to follow through on commitments; your heart is open to receive with appropriate boundaries; you are authentic in your communication; you look clearly and objectively at your thought patterns and habits; and you listen to the quiet place inside.

When this happens, what you believe, think, say, and do line up, and you can manifest what you want in your life. You are in sync with your body, your mind, and source energy, which connects you to all life and the energy of the universe. It is through this, your connection to universal energy, that you are able to manifest your desires and work on deeply healing physical, mental, and emotional wounds.

Universal Energy

Universal energy is the energy that creates life. The sun, water, and all living beings are made of energy. Therefore, all things communicate and affect each other. Your thoughts are energy, and they affect the path of your life and the makeup of your body, the basic units of which are atoms, or energy.

In today's fast-paced world, it's common not to focus on health until something goes wrong. It seems normal to keep going and going until you feel an ache or pain, and then you visit a doctor. Until a physical sign affects the way you perform your daily activities, it's easy to ignore how you're feeling. Maintaining good health should be an ongoing practice, however, not something to wait to do until you're already showing physical symptoms of disease. Chakra healing can be done regularly, as part of your ongoing self-care practice, and this will be both a proactive and a preventative way to take care of yourself and bring more joy into your life.

Healing the energetic centers is the key to overall health because they are connected to everything else about you. If you treat signs of disease only in your physical body, the blocks and traumas that are stored in your energy body will eventually cause more physical disease. This is what chakra healing on all levels refers to: unblocking and balancing the flow of energy for the health of your body, mind, and spirit.

According to chakra theory, imprints of your karma from past lives are stored in the chakras. By working with the chakras, you are not just clearing wounds you've accumulated since your birth in this life, you are also working with past lifetimes of karma. The body dies, and the energy system carries karma from one life to the next. Working on clearing the chakras is a way to keep evolving toward becoming a light in the world.

GETTING TO KNOW YOURSELF

The first step of chakra healing is to learn to become aware of how you are feeling physically, mentally, and emotionally moment to moment. Slow down during your day, and this will help you get used to paying attention to how you are. When you notice yourself dashing from one place to the next, losing your keys, or having ten different to-do lists, it's a perfect time to realize you must slow down. On the other hand, if you are someone who doesn't feel rushed and busy, if you are instead feeling too static and bored, that is a good thing to notice as well.

CHECKING IN WITH YOURSELF

At least a few times per day, take a moment to pause and notice how you are feeling. Are you tired, worried, bored, or frustrated? Are you happy, grateful, productive, or content? At what points in the day does your state of mind shift, if at all? Make it a practice to begin to notice how you are feeling during your days and nights. How are you feeling right now? Notice. Do not judge your feelings as good or bad. Just notice. For example, if you feel anxious during the day, the first step is to notice without labeling it "bad" or "good." You'll come to see that labels aren't useful, and how you are feeling during the day affects your body. Noticing how you are feeling, in specific ways, will help illuminate how to proceed with chakra healing and will help you notice the benefits.

Align Your Care

Being in contact with a professional therapist or doctor, especially when you start a new healing process, is always a good idea. While the practices in this book can be done by yourself, when it comes to your health, always check in with professionally trained and reputable doctors, therapists, and energy healers as you progress.

You might need to mindfully unplug from technology as you start to check in on how you feel over the course of a day. Remove the distractions so you can accurately assess your physical, mental, and emotional states.

THE HIDDEN SIDES OF YOU

One important piece of chakra healing involves being willing to get to know yourself in the way you show up in the world—the sides of you that you might feel proud of as well as the sides of you that you might find unbearable to admit, the shadow sides. For healing to occur, it is important that you allow all sides of you to come to light, so you can work with them.

In order to allow things to surface, keep an open mind and let any judgments gently float away. In the yogic tradition, this includes being open to seeing your good and bad karma, so you can make amends in the ways that are necessary to break free from your particular karmic patterns.

It might be hard to admit to your shadow sides, and so it might be hard for you to even know what they are. One way to notice your shadow sides is to reflect on times when someone does something that bothers you. Why does it bother you? Now take some time and ask yourself if you ever do the same thing to others. You might not realize or think you do, but give it a few days or a week of awareness. Keep your eye out to see if you do that same thing that bothers you. Often others provide mirrors for us of our patterns, without us being aware enough to notice. Now dig deep and ask yourself, *Why do you do that thing you can't bear when you see it in someone else? What is it in you that causes you to do that?* It's possible that you are protecting yourself in some way. Ask yourself if you are ready to drop the fear and attachment to that pattern, and if not, what is holding you back?

CHAKRA HEALING CAN BALANCE YOUR LIFE FORCE

The chakra system circulates energy, the same life-force energy that illuminates the sky and creates life on earth. When the chakras are blocked, they are not giving and receiving life-force energy in a balanced way. This imbalance correlates directly to your psychological and physical states. Each chakra creates, aggravates, and ameliorates certain psychological issues and physical symptoms, and by noticing how you feel, you can decide which chakras need healing work.

Balance All Your Chakras

Balancing all the chakras is better than focusing on just one chakra. All the chakras are connected, and the life-force energy needs to be able to travel all the way up and all the way down for your optimum health and vitality. For quick fixes, you can focus on one or two of the chakras, but later take time to balance them all.

If you need practice feeling your life-force energy, try this simple exercise. Hold your arms out to the sides and rapidly wiggle your fingers and shake your hands in the air. Shake and wave your hands. Count to thirty as you do this. Then suddenly stop. Notice what you feel. Do you feel a tingling? Do you feel vibration? That's life-force energy.

Spend more time evaluating your energy level. Spend time noticing how others make you feel. Who in your life fills you up? Who makes you feel tired? It's not always just what they say or how they say it; people's energy fields interact with yours. If you feel like someone drains your energy, you might not be able to spend a lot of time with that person. By the same token, you can be nourished by another's healing energy.

The purpose of having this research available is to notice how different systems of thought can work together for overall healing. If you already work with the meridians, there might be ways that you can use this information to enhance your chakra healing practices.

CHAKRA HEALING THROUGH ACUPUNCTURE AND MERIDIANS

The chakra system is connected to major lines of energy in the body called nadis. The life force that flows through these is called *prana* in Sanskrit. Prana is the same as the flow of energy in Chinese medicine called *chi* and in Japanese *qi*. If you practice tai chi or qigong, you are accustomed to working with that energy.

Chinese acupuncture is based on the desire to help chi flow freely throughout the body. The practice of acupuncture is to place tiny hair-thin needles on acupressure points to stimulate certain meridians that connect to different organs of the body. Meridians are energy channels that connect hands, feet, head, and all body parts together.

Acupuncture is a treatment that you receive repeatedly, even if for the same condition. Many people experience relief immediately, but because energy is always shifting and reacting to other energetic stimuli, acupuncture treatment is something that is scheduled on a regular basis to help continue to balance energy flow over time. The results of a single treatment aren't usually permanent.

In Paul Grilley's DVD on the chakras, he gives a straightforward list of which chakras control energy flow through which meridians. Grilley's list is based on the work of Dr. Hiroshi Motoyama. The correlations are shown in the following table, with the primary meridians being the ones most strongly affected by their corresponding chakras.

Chakras and Corresponding Meridians		
Chakra	Primary Meridians	Secondary Meridians
Root	Kidney and urinary bladder	Small intestine, liver, and triple heater
Sacral	Kidney and urinary bladder	Small intestine, liver, and triple heater
Solar Plexus	Stomach, spleen, liver, and gall bladder	Large intestine and small intestine
Heart	Heart and small intestine	Heart constrictor
Throat	Lung and large intestine	Heart constrictor
Third Eye	Governor vessel and conception vessel	Urinary bladder and small intestine
Crown	Governor vessel and conception vessel	Urinary bladder and small intestine

From Paul Grilley, *Chakra Theory and Meditation.*

COMBINING CHAKRA HEALING AND MODERN MEDICINE

The US National Institutes of Health (NIH) is the nation's medical research branch. It researches and explains important discoveries that improve health. The NIH recognizes the healing power of complementary and alternative healing practices for health, including yoga, meditation, acupuncture, tai chi, and qigong. All of these practices work with your energy body, addressing vital parts of you that allopathic medicine—the use of drugs and surgery—does not.

The NIH has a branch called the National Center for Complementary and Integrative Health (NCCIH). The NCCIH presents information as well as conducts and funds research on the efficacy of complementary and alternative medicine. The existence of this branch of the NIH is recognition that patients are very interested in complementary healing modalities, and doctors are interested in finding viable solutions to health concerns. Many people want to read scientific data before diving into another type of treatment, unless they've already tried everything allopathic and realize they need to be treated with other therapies. So, as NCCIH can provide scientific statistics, it will help inform people of the potential of these other forms of healing. To see the NCCIH's latest information, visit https://nccih.nih.gov.

Chakra healing complements modern medicine well because it's not physically invasive and doesn't have the negative side effects that many drugs do. Even still, as always, before embarking on any new activities, it's important to talk to a doctor who understands clearly the medications you are on and how additional therapies might interact with them. One way to understand how chakra healing can complement modern medicine is as a way of intentionally directing the effects of your yoga, meditation, and prayer practices.

Integrative Doctors

Doctors who recommend allopathic treatment as well as complementary and alternative therapies are called integrative. So ask around for recommendations or do an online search for a reputable integrative doctor.

After learning about the chakra healing journey, you may decide to find an integrative doctor as your primary care physician. A wonderful integrative doctor will feel absolutely comfortable recommending pain medication and other necessary allopathic treatments. He or she also will believe in your choice to add complementary support such as meditation, vitamins, and massage into your plan for healing, and can help you come up with a plan suitable for where you are in your healing process.

CHAPTER 3

CHAKRA HEALING BENEFITS

Physical disturbances such as headaches, fatigue, and stomachaches are symptoms of disease that begin in your subtle energy body before manifesting as disease or pain in your physical body. If you treat only physical symptoms, those symptoms will return unless you address the imprints in your energy field. Those imprints can occur at birth, or even earlier. By healing your chakras, you are working on deep healing that lies beneath the physical pain. In this chapter, we'll look at some of the specific benefits of chakra healing.

ENCOURAGE OVERALL WELL-BEING

It's a tall order to ask for overall well-being, but healing the chakras can live up to that request if you dedicate yourself to the art. When you are motivated to improve yourself, you can truly enjoy the process. At the same time, healing the chakras will likely bring up difficult memories and emotions that you've been repressing or suppressing because they felt too big to deal with. To heal on a deep level, you must care about what's happening in your subtle energy system. The subtle energy system works in tandem with your physical body and psychology, so unblocking energy flow can restore you on psychological, physical, and mental levels.

ALLEVIATE SUFFERING

Chakra theory exists to help you navigate the journey of healing on all levels, and ultimately this means healing from all suffering. If you want to be free of suffering entirely, according to yoga philosophy you would transcend what the yogis call the cycle of samsara that includes birth, death, and rebirth.

Yogis believe you return lifetime after lifetime in physical form to work through your karma. Some karma affects your life in a way that will feel helpful to you, and some affects your life in a way that will make you feel uncomfortable. The sincerely beneficial, positive things you do for others and the world will come back to you in the same way. If you are dishonest or if you act in a way that is not harmonious in the world, when that karma comes back to you it will make you uncomfortable. In this view, what goes around comes around.

Chakra Healing Complements Any Belief System

Anyone can benefit from chakra healing. In fact, you can use chakra healing with any belief system. Chakra healing gives you the opportunity to examine your patterns and health now, and learn which chakras correlate to your habits and symptoms. Then, by balancing the chakras that are out of balance, you can work on healing starting today.

To get beyond this cycle is to transcend the cycle of samsara, not identify at all with a physical body or the pleasures and pain of the world, and merge with the oneness of the universal energy. There isn't an easy how-to manual on that process of liberation, but the *Yoga Sutras* by Patanjali is a guide. Because of its relationship to prana (the flow of energy), chakra meditation is a useful place to begin your quest to reduce suffering.

BRING AUTHENTIC SELF-AWARENESS

As you study your chakras and work to balance them, you will become more and more aware of who you truly are. You will notice yourself as an energetic being with unique gifts and wounds. You will look openly and with courage at where you close off in life, where you are open, and where you feel stuck. You will be able to see these habits in your-self and decide to practice letting them go.

As you uncover your habits and patterns, you will discover where you need to loosen up. In other words, you will learn where you can loosen your energetic grip on ways of being that really do not serve you. The easiest way is to begin to notice where your thoughts often go, what you focus on, who and what angers and upsets you, what brings you joy, what makes you tired, what gives you energy, what you wish for, and what you resent. As you sort out which things light you up in your life, you begin to acknowledge what your gifts are. And from there you can realize your dharma, how you can best contribute to the world. This is authentic self-awareness.

ILLUMINATE YOUR LIFE PATH

Chakra healing can be a huge support as you discover and follow your life's purpose. When you do grounding practices for the Root Chakra to keep it in balance, your body will feel grounded. When the body feels grounded, your mind calms down. As you move up the chakras and balance the Sacral Chakra, you enliven your ability to go with the flow. You might need to accept some upcoming change, and this helps you adapt. Moving up to the Solar Plexus Chakra, you stoke the fire of will, self-esteem, and stamina. Healing the Heart Chakra will help you in your connections with others; perhaps they'll give advice and wisdom. A balanced Throat Chakra will help you stay true to yourself, when choices arise. The Third Eye Chakra will be your connection to your wisdom. And when you meditate on the Crown Chakra you'll experience the calm feeling of oneness that restores you on this journey.

IMPROVE RELATIONSHIPS

Whether in partnership, companionship, marriage, friendship, or relationships with coworkers, working on chakra healing will help you in your connections with others. You will:

* Feel more balanced, so you will be less needy and know you are supported.
* Be able to put things in perspective when conflicts arise.
* Become aware of which people in your life are not good for you.
* Attract the types of people you want in your life.
* Have the courage to initiate important conversations.
* Have a healthy sex drive.
* Become a good listener.

Chakra healing helps you in relationships because you will understand that you and others are energetic beings. You will understand that you have your own energetic blocks as does the other person. You will notice how your energy complements the energy of another, and how your energies mix in difficult ways. And with this knowledge, you can step back, take a breath, and have a conversation about what you are noticing.

Chakra healing can strengthen your courage to have a difficult conversation with another person by helping you stay in the place of compassion and curiosity, knowing that your interpretation and the other person's will likely be very different. It's important to come to the talk with tenderness, even if you're feeling hurt. And, if you are on the other end of such a conversation, try to really hear what the other person is saying. Try listening, without reacting, to what their experience is. And, you could work together to find a solution of how to stop the hurtful pattern. In relationships, listening is an invaluable skill to practice.

PROMOTE INTIMACY

When you work with chakra healing, you will notice which chakras are blocked. Creating intimacy requires energy from all chakras: the trust in safety of the Root, the sexual intimacy of the Sacral, the fire and passion of the Solar Plexus, the tenderness of the Heart, the openness of the Throat, the connection to each other on the level of intuition at the Third Eye, and the connection to the bliss energy through the Crown.

When you are intimate with another person, sometimes the energy of their chakras can help awaken one of yours. Or, if you both are balanced in the same chakras, they can give and receive well to each other. If you both are blocked at the same chakra, the relationship may struggle until you realize where you are blocked and can talk about it and deal with it compassionately and patiently.

PROVIDE THE JOY OF SELF-CARE

Taking care of yourself can be a pleasure, and you deserve it. You will be more productive, a brighter light, and a support in the world if you take time out each day to take care of yourself.

Get up early enough to have time to do a morning routine. At the very least, before jumping out of bed, take a moment to pause. Take a few breaths. Allow yourself to wake up in bed. Do a few easy, simple stretches. When you get out of bed, make sure you have time to eat a good breakfast, brush and floss your teeth, and step outside for a breath of fresh air before moving on with your busy day.

It's important to eat healthily as well. When grocery shopping, pick out foods in all the colors of the rainbow. Ask friends and coworkers if they have any favorite recipes for the season and swap. Take pleasure in trying new things, and seeing how many different colors you can eat in one day.

When you take care of yourself, you're helping yourself and those around you. By being healthy you are a light for others, and a model of how good health can look and feel. As you become healthy, others will wonder how you did it. Taking pleasure in taking care of yourself allows others to see that it's possible and to feel all right doing the same. And, when you are healthy, you have the energy and ability to give back.

DE-STRESS

One of the best overarching benefits of chakra healing is that you can manage your life with more ease and less stress. This happens because life-force energy flows through your chakras in an appropriate way, and the energy spreads throughout your entire body. Energy affects psychological and physical functions, and because it's life-force energy, it is good for you. It's the energy of creation, of transformation, of life.

Chakra healing has the potential to create more ease in your life. When you work with the chakras, you are following yogic and meditative practices that are designed to remove your mind from fixation on worries or stress. You are cultivating witness consciousness, whereby you'll see things just as they are without adding extra drama. By practicing creating less of a drama in your mind, you will create space to feel more ease around things as they come up. In addition, you are bringing energy into the body with these healing practices, which can help feed parts of you that feel depleted or shut down. Having more energy can make your day easier and more peaceful.

Finding peace comes first from within. If you feel as though you are constantly struggling, it's time to relax. At your very core, in stillness, there is peace. If you aren't used to accessing it, it will take some practice.

Chakra healing helps bring peace to your life because you are allowing the life force to flow freely through the body's energy channels, supporting the body's endocrine system and sympathetic nervous system. When those are supported and they do not have to work overtime, then at appropriate times you can rest and your parasympathetic nervous system will become engaged. When your body is not in fight-or-flight mode, overworking the sympathetic nervous system, your body has time to restore itself. And as the body restores, you can feel at peace. If energy is flowing well through the body, it's much easier to feel peaceful than it is when energy is blocked.

Feeling safe can help you de-stress as well. If you don't feel secure or safe at home or supported by family or friends, your mind is occupied with that until you can make a change. This change may require a combination of responses from you, which could include changing your attitude, realizing in what ways you are safe, or—if you aren't physically and emotionally safe—taking action and reaching out for guidance and help. If you are living in a safe home, and if you have food to sustain you and clothing to keep you warm, it's important to work on your Root Chakra to help you feel safe in a world of uncertainty.

Accessing joy is a healthy part of a peaceful life. When you feel lighter and joyful, your body can function in its normal way without being tight from worry, or working extra hard to deal with the effects of stress. The way to joy through the chakra journey comes from the meditative and healing practices that you do, and the open attitude that you bring. Think of bringing a childlike curiosity, wonder, and innocence to the process.

Ease Your Mind

As you get started with chakra healing practice, you might question whether you are "doing it right," perhaps asking yourself, *What happens if I send healing energy to the wrong chakra?* There's no need to worry. If you end up sending healing energy to a chakra that is already in balance, it will not have negative effects. All of the chakras will benefit from nourishing practices. The chakras all affect each other, so sending healing energy to any of them will work well.

Chakra healing is a positive thing for your mind, body, and spirit. Enter it with gentleness and patience. It's essential for you to go gently and pay attention to how your body responds. Do not do anything that will cause you pain or seems too much for you. Gently and carefully cultivate this relationship with your energy system and you will notice your life unfolding with less stress.

CHAPTER 4

HEALING POWERS OF SPECIFIC CHAKRAS

When the chakras are functioning well, they will support your psychological equilibrium, your mental functioning, and your physical health. But you'll need to know which chakras relate to which physical and mental conditions so you can work on them appropriately. This chapter explains the connections that each chakra has to specific organs and body parts, as well as the links between each chakra and the energy of certain psychological patterns. As with all medical issues, speak to your integrative health specialist about the best ways to treat yourself before proceeding.

CHAKRAS' RELATIONSHIPS TO ENDOCRINE FUNCTIONS

Energy from the chakras affects the glands of the endocrine system, which initiate essential biochemical processes. If you notice you have an imbalance in your physical body that relates to any gland in the endocrine system, then you can trace that function to a specific chakra. Working on that chakra will then balance the energy flow to that gland and support its proper function.

Alice Bailey and Charles Webster Leadbeater, both Theosophists (see Chapter 1), were the first to notice that energy from the chakras affects the endocrine and sympathetic nervous systems of the body. Their discoveries paved the way for today's continually unfolding understanding of how the chakras affect and respond to chemical and physical actions and reactions in the body. Each chakra flowers out from the spine toward ductless glands of the endocrine system, affecting the production of hormones that run through the body.

Each gland affects certain bodily functions, and therefore if you notice what's not functioning well, you can trace it to a particular chakra or chakras. Knowing these relationships will help direct your healing practices. The endocrine system, like all systems of the body, is complicated. Science can explain certain functions, though it doesn't yet claim to understand everything about how the endocrine system works. Because there are so many unknowns about the mind and body, you should explore all potential avenues toward healing; supplementing allopathic treatments with your own visualizations, intentions, and attention can help speed up the process and increase positive outcomes. Following is more information about how specific chakras interact with your endocrine system.

THE ROOT CHAKRA AND THE GONADS

The Root Chakra affects the gonads, and in some traditions, the adrenals. The gonads are the glands that are closest to the earth. These are responsible for the production of the hormones that determine the secondary physical characteristics associated with male and female and fertility. The hormones are testosterone, progesterone, and estrogen. If you have troubles from improper secretion and functions of these hormones, work on your lower chakras. The first and second chakras' energies support the gonads.

THE SACRAL CHAKRA AND THE ADRENALS

The Sacral Chakra affects the adrenals, and in some traditions, the gonads. The adrenals balance the body's response to stress, including regulating your metabolism and supporting your immune system. The adrenals get activated in the fight-or-flight response, regulating the hormones adrenaline, cortisol, and aldosterone. If you are often in the fight-or-flight response, your body doesn't have time to revitalize and nourish itself. Balancing the lower chakras will help ground you and bring you out of this condition that is meant just for times when you really need it.

If, for example, you're in fight-or-flight more often than relaxation, take the time to figure out why. Is it based mainly on external factors? Is it predominantly psychological? Look into the causes and work on ameliorating them. In addition, find ways to add relaxation into your life. In relaxation, your body recovers from the work, thinking, and moving that you do all day. Relaxation is restorative, and helps the body perform its functions.

In addition to relaxation, balancing the lowest three chakras can help get you out of the fight-or-flight response. For example, if you're in fight-or-flight often because you're experiencing a lot of change, bringing energy to the Root Chakra will help stabilize and ground you. Working on the Sacral Chakra will help you relax around the changes and be more fluid. And the Solar Plexus Chakra will give you fire and courage to feel self-confident as you ride these waves of change. Energizing these chakras, because of their location, will send energy to the adrenals to support them while you're dealing with so much change. A combination of energizing your chakras and getting enough rest will help your body stay healthier in stressful times.

If you're under stress for a period of time, it can cause your adrenals to work overtime and need some support. Stress will have a domino effect, causing other glands of the endocrine system to overwork. Energizing all of the chakras will support the function of the gonads and adrenals, which work together with all the glands in the endocrine system.

THE SOLAR PLEXUS CHAKRA AND THE PANCREAS

The Solar Plexus Chakra affects the cells in the pancreas called the islets of Langerhans, and the adrenals. The islets of Langerhans cells in the pancreas are responsible for secreting insulin, which metabolizes sugar. Dysfunction here can result in diabetes. Because of its location in the body, the third chakra's energy flowers out toward the pancreas. A blocked third chakra could affect the functions of your pancreas over time.

THE HEART CHAKRA AND THE THYMUS

The Heart Chakra, which flowers out from the center of the sternum, affects the thymus, an endocrine system gland that is located in the upper chest. The thymus produces T-cells that recognize when something foreign is in the body. Loss of function of the thymus hinders the body's ability to fight infection. The Heart Chakra's energy radiates outward toward this gland, so hindrances to the energy flow can negatively influence thymus function.

THE THROAT CHAKRA AND THE THYROID

The Throat Chakra is associated with the thyroid and parathyroid glands, which are located in the neck. The Throat Chakra energy flowers out toward these glands. Troubles with the thyroid, whether hyperthyroidism or hypothyroidism, can lead to weight problems, sore throat, and difficulty swallowing. If you have a thyroid condition, pay attention to the Throat Chakra when you do your healing practices.

THE THIRD EYE AND CROWN CHAKRAS AND THE PITUITARY AND PINEAL GLANDS

The upper two chakras are both near the brain, near the pituitary and the pineal glands. Traditions differ on which chakra links with which gland. In any case, well-balanced energy in both the Third Eye Chakra and the Crown Chakra will help ensure proper functioning of these vital parts of the endocrine system. The pituitary gland is thought to control and regulate the function of all of the glands. The pineal gland secretes melatonin in response to darkness; it helps regulate your sleeping schedule. If you're having trouble sleeping, gently massage the top of your head and then the third eye. Bring awareness to those areas. Do this for several minutes, imagining relaxation and serenity floating from your fingertips deep into your mind.

THE CHAKRAS AND PSYCHOLOGY

One of the most obvious ways to evaluate which chakras are imbalanced is to pay attention to how you're doing psychologically. The energy of certain psychological patterns has been traced to particular chakras. When you notice which patterns you're exhibiting in your life, you can work on balancing the energy of the corresponding chakra and the chakras directly above and below.

The following table shows you which chakra to work on when you're experiencing specific issues:

Chakra	Corresponds with issues relating to…
Root	Security, safety, and stability
Sacral	Creating and adapting to change
Solar Plexus	Self-esteem, will power, and transformation
Heart	Being expansive
Throat	Being authentically you
Third Eye	Seeing beyond the physical
Crown	Connecting to the Divine

Read on for more specific information about each.

ROOT CHAKRA: SECURITY, SAFETY, AND STABILITY

The issues of the Root Chakra concern your basic needs. Do you have a safe home as well as money for food and clothes? If your basic needs are met, it's important to notice if you feel safe, secure, and stable. Your sense of security, safety, and stability comes from within, once you do have enough resources to live a comfortable life. At times when you truly do not have a home, food, or clothing then your thoughts will understandably be preoccupied with getting those for yourself. You instinctively need those basics.

At times when you have your needs met, then check to see if you still feel unstable in relationship to your basic necessities. If you still feel unstable, this could be a pattern imprinted in your energy field. A sense of real security comes from within; it's not about money. It's the belief that you have the right to be alive. It is in believing that you are worthy of loving and being loved. Your sense of security stems from the recognition that your life isn't an accident or a mistake, and that you aren't a burden on the planet. You can shine and be seen, heard, and appreciated. And you deserve to have money, a home, a car, and the pleasures that life offers. If you aren't secure in your right to exist, to be safe and content, then you will not feel stable, safe, and secure even with enough money. You will never feel safe until you address those deeper issues of your basic right to be alive and well. You can support yourself and strengthen such beliefs by working with the Root Chakra.

Balance Chakras to Find Focus

If you feel "spacey" or unable to focus, work on balancing your lower chakras. In particular, start with the energy center closest to earth: the Root. Balancing the Root Chakra will help bring you out of the clouds and back down to earth.

Because all the chakras work together, if one isn't working well it will affect the others. If you're feeling unsafe and insecure, you will not have the energy for other aspects of your life such as being productive at work or being open to loving relationships. Dealing with the psychological issues of the first chakra will form a base support for all else in your life. When your Root Chakra is balanced you are able to see tasks through to completion, you feel supported, and you feel safe in your day-to-day life.

DEALING WITH ANXIETY

If you have feelings of anxiety, you can get help from the Root Chakra. When you are anxious your mind will spin in circles of worry.

You also might notice physical effects: your heart may beat faster, your breath may become shallow, and your belly may become upset. Chronic anxiety can lead to various physical symptoms and disease.

When you are anxious your energy is predominantly up in your mind. So, you want to bring your energy down. Doing something physical, energizing the body, will bring energy down from the mind into the body. If the weather permits, get outside to allow the earth's force to help ground you. Whether or not you can get outside, breathe in and out slowly, gently, and deeply, feeling your body expand to allow the air to rush inward on the inhale. Envision your connection to the earth, as you imagine your inhale going through your body into the ground. Create longer exhalation than inhalation to induce relaxation. If you are standing up, imagine your legs as though they have roots growing deeply into the earth. Know you are rooted and connected. If you want to sit down on the ground or floor, then you can imagine the energy coming down from your head out through the Root Chakra into the earth. For several minutes, breathe and envision energy coming down into the body and flowing into the earth.

Stomping to Release Stress

Stomping your feet is a great way to ground. If you stomp outside, you leave the energy out there. Let it go. You can even stomp your feet outside each day after work, before entering your home. Even if you love your job, this will allow you to not bring work stress into the house.

If you recognize that anxiety is common in your life, add more physical activity into your day. If your tendency is to be thinking all of the time or if your job requires a lot of brainpower, make sure you take some physical movement breaks. Literally move your body. This could mean putting in your earbuds and dancing for a song (even at your desk), or while you're sitting down giving your face, arms, legs, and back a massage. At the very least you could stand up and take a walk down the hall or outside for a five-minute breath of air. Taking a five- or ten-minute break every hour or two during your day will not slow you down—it will help your productivity.

When you're taking a break to move, bring your awareness and attention into your body. If you're walking, feel your legs moving and standing on the ground; ground that energy. If you're doing a self-massage, notice how your muscles feel. And don't worry that if you stop you won't be able to think again. Leave yourself a note about what you were doing, and when you return, your energy will be able to go back up into your mind and start working again. This is very healthy; it will give your mind a much-needed break, and help you practice grounding your energy so when anxiety arises you can ground yourself.

ATTENTION DEFICIT HYPERACTIVITY DISORDER (ADHD)

Chakra healing activities and therapy that focus on issues associated with the Root Chakra could complement traditional treatments for attention deficit hyperactivity disorder (ADHD). ADHD is characterized by restlessness, inability to focus, and impulsive behavior. The grounding quality of a balanced Root Chakra that connects the body and mind to the earth could create a sense of comfort in being still and focusing.

CREATING FINANCIAL ABUNDANCE

You have the right to have money and to have success in any area of your life you choose. It's okay to have money, it's okay to be successful, and it's okay to work in a job you enjoy. If you have a deficient

Root Chakra, you may be prone to fear that can affect your aspirations to acquire or hold onto what you need. You may associate different fears with accumulating what you want. On top of not believing you deserve it, it's possible you will be afraid of what might happen if you do become successful or have exactly what you want.

Fear can be a very useful part of your life. It will allow you to be cautious and examine risks and potential pitfalls as you make decisions in your life. If you stick in that zone, though, of fearing the potential pitfalls rather than moving ahead and giving new things a try, then you are being ruled by a deficiency in the Root Chakra. When you work to unblock this chakra, you are unleashing your cosmic ability to bring your dreams to reality. The results of bringing new projects to fruition, entering new relationships, acquiring money, and improving your physical health become reality with the energy of this chakra.

EATING WELL

If your Root Chakra is underactive, you may notice you aren't eating enough and are losing weight. One way you might respond to this energy imbalance is to overeat to help you feel grounded. It's true that eating can help ground you, so it's a valid physical response. In the long run, though, overeating is not good for your body, nor is eating for emotional reasons good for your soul. If you notice your eating habits aren't healthy for you, try Root Chakra–balancing exercises (described in Part 2) and mentally check in with yourself to see if you can address what makes you feel unsafe.

CLINGING

If you notice you have clinging patterns, your Root Chakra could be acting excessively to compensate for its imbalance. To try to feel more stable, you cling to people and possessions. Clinging behavior will cause people to pull away, which will leave you feeling more ungrounded. If you notice yourself acting this way, it's a sign of an unbalanced Root Chakra.

SACRAL CHAKRA: CREATING AND ADAPTING TO CHANGE

The health of your Sacral Chakra shows up in your emotional stability, sexuality, creativity, attitude toward pleasure, and relationship to going with the flow of life. Being able to enjoy dancing, having sex, creating, and trying new experiences all relate to the second chakra. If you feel guilty when you think about taking pleasure in life, if no new activities interest you, or if you can't enjoy the sensations in your body (including massage or dancing), then it's likely that energy isn't flowing steadily through this second chakra.

Enjoying Your Hobbies

A healthy relationship to pleasure is when you can enjoy yourself and feel satisfied afterward. For example, you can enjoy going dancing for a few hours, and also you could live without it. It means that your ability to feel emotionally balanced isn't dependent on that pleasurable activity, and it's not your way of avoiding reality.

As one of the lower chakras, the Sacral Chakra is associated with feeling stable. Being able to go with the flow or explore something new with creativity is also related to how secure you feel. If you aren't feeling as though you are basically safe, supported, and allowed to be as you are, then trying new things will be incredibly difficult if at all possible. When your second chakra is balanced, you enjoy taking pleasure in life, you can tap into your creative juices, and you have a healthy relationship to your sexuality.

ADDICTION AND REPRESSION

Addiction is associated with an unbalanced Sacral Chakra. If you don't have a healthy relationship to pleasure, it can turn into addiction. In this case, perhaps you feel as though you can't get enough of what you have been denied or what you think you shouldn't do. So you are compelled to desire it, to have it, or to experience it over and over. This can show up as obsessive behavior and reinforce itself in a guilt-filled indulgent pattern of behavior. Guilt shows up here because you are denied something pleasurable, and then it can become exacerbated when you allow yourself to have it. Addiction can be a sign that the Sacral Chakra is reacting excessively.

On the other hand, if you are completely withdrawn from pleasure, creativity, and sensation, then this chakra is deficient. Both are blocked conditions; it's just that the exercises you choose to unblock the chakra will differ based on whether you're dealing with an excessive or deficient chakra.

SWEETNESS

A literal translation of *Svadhisthana* is "sweetness," and when this Sacral Chakra is balanced you feel at ease enjoying life's pleasures. You relax when taking a hot bath. You smile when eating ice cream. You intentionally rub the flannel sheet against your cheek when pulling up the covers. You experience intimacy with your sexual partners. These all are moments that are pleasurable, and your enjoyment helps balance your Sacral Chakra.

SOLAR PLEXUS CHAKRA: SELF-ESTEEM, WILL POWER, AND TRANSFORMATION

The Solar Plexus Chakra is your personal power center. When you're feeling secure about what you have to offer, when you can turn challenges into opportunities, and when you feel good about offering your ideas to others, energy is flowing well through this third chakra.

A common quality that challenges this chakra's flow is shame. If you deal with issues around shame, bringing energy to the Solar Plexus Chakra will be a helpful piece of your practice. If you avoid confrontation, or if you isolate yourself from the world, working with this chakra could be very supportive for you.

DEPRESSION AND CHRONIC FATIGUE

Depression and chronic fatigue can be symptoms of a weak Solar Plexus Chakra. A functioning third chakra is associated with an appropriate amount of energy and enthusiasm for moving forward in life; a deficient chakra shows less will for living, doing, and participating. In those cases, energy moves sluggishly through this chakra, which isn't supportive of its element: fire.

Self-Reflection

A healthy dose of fire is essential, but pay attention to see if you have an excessive Solar Plexus Chakra. Are you secure sharing the spotlight and tasks, or are you demanding and overbearing? If the answer is the latter, you could be compensating for a weak Solar Plexus Chakra. Knowing the difference will help you tailor your healing process.

If you experience depression, working on bringing more energy to the Solar Plexus Chakra can help. Sometimes, be aware that perhaps you need rest. If you've been overdoing it, the body and mind could use solid downtime. Exhaustion can be the result of numerous things, so when your body calls for rest allow yourself time to rest. Especially if you know you're dealing with a lot and juggling many obligations in your life, of course you will need time to recharge. If you find that your need for sleep hinders your day-to-day activities, that's when you should talk to someone about it, and also try the energizing Solar Plexus Chakra activities (see Part 2). You also may need a combination of both restorative and energizing activities in your day. You can stoke your Manipura fire, as well as make sure you're giving your body and mind the rest they call for.

Depression can also be associated with the Heart Chakra. Because a deficient Heart Chakra can cause you to feel isolated and alone, depression can follow. Bringing energy to both the Solar Plexus Chakra and the Heart Chakra could be very helpful complements to your other treatments for depression.

ANGER

A lot of anger reveals an excessive Solar Plexus Chakra. Other symptoms are being judgmental, impatient, and controlling. If these are qualities you relate to, an important part of your practice will be the methods that balance an overactive Solar Plexus Chakra.

MOTIVATION FOR YOUR HEALING JOURNEY

When energy flows well through the Solar Plexus Chakra it will help you with your entire healing process. Willpower will help you stick to your practices, good self-esteem will remind you that you're worth it, and the transformative energy will help you literally transform. Take good care of this chakra, as you do with all of them, because it will help you push through the sluggish doldrums that you may sometimes feel. And, when energy flows freely here, it will help you initiate projects or changes in your life you've been wanting.

HEART CHAKRA: BEING EXPANSIVE

The Heart Chakra is tender and sensitive. It perceives the energy of others, and gathers information. If your Heart Chakra is blocked, it not only prevents you from giving love, it stops you from feeling love. In this case, the Heart Chakra is protected in its closed-off state, and it cannot receive.

HEART CONNECTION

When your heart is open to receive the energy of another living being, information is exchanged that goes beyond what words can convey. You may never be able to put it into words, and it wouldn't matter. There is a felt sense of communication between two friends, family members, and lovers when the heart space is open that doesn't need to be expressed in any other way. You may feel it as warmth, you may feel it as joy, you may feel it as support. However it feels in your physical body, you know that your hearts are communicating with each other and exchanging nourishing energy.

In instances when the Heart Chakra shuts down, you can reopen it with healing practices just as you can open all of the chakras. Though the heart is sensitive, it is also strong. It can recover from heartache if you nurture it.

TRUE LOVE

Love at the Heart Chakra is different from the sexual love felt in the Sacral Chakra. Love at the Heart Chakra is unconditional, it doesn't have to be between lovers, and it lifts your spirit. There's acceptance, support, joy, respect, and true care between people whose Heart Chakras are both open to each other. It's a feeling of peace and harmony like no other, and it continues to create good feelings such as spaciousness, acceptance, and ease. An important aspect of this type of love is also self-love, self-acceptance.

Like any other chakra, the Heart Chakra can be excessive. If you are so vehemently expressing your love and not pausing or relaxing, you cannot take in love. In this case, it would help to use chakra healing to transfer the excessive energy into other chakras, leaving space in the Heart Chakra to receive.

THROAT CHAKRA: BEING AUTHENTICALLY YOU

The Throat Chakra is the energy behind self-expression. This is the chakra that allows you to express your true feelings, wants, and needs. While you need the proper functioning of all the chakras, when your Throat Chakra is imbalanced you will have trouble with relationships socially and professionally. This chakra relates to your communication skills.

LEARNING TO ASK FOR SUPPORT

Others won't know what you need or how things are really going for you if you are unable to tell them. At work, this could lead you to burn out, if you are unable to clearly and appropriately ask for the help you need.

In relationships, those who love you will not know what makes you feel supported, what hurts you, and how to work together, if you avoid having the hard conversations. If you are unable to express your truth, you could become resentful of others and frustrated. Understandably, from their perspective, if they don't know what you really want or need, how could they support you? In your efforts to not rock the boat, you'll deny others the benefit of your viewpoint. The effect is that you may choose to leave relationships or jobs rather than have the conversations that could actually make things much better.

Activating Your Throat Chakra

One way to energize your Throat Chakra is to hum or sing more often. If you don't want to sing in front of others, sing in the shower or sing in the car. If someone drives by and notices, you might inspire her to do the same.

Just as speaking your truth will allow others to support you, it will allow you to support them. When you are supported and heard, you can focus your energy on the tasks at hand rather than losing energy to emotions or blocks that come up because you're not saying what needs to be said.

LISTEN CAREFULLY

If you talk often, rapidly, or loudly, your Throat Chakra might be excessive. One of the ways to calm your energy down is to set an intention to listen more often and more carefully. Reassure yourself that you will get your turn to talk, if not today, then next time. With an excessive Throat Chakra, you might feel you need to keep talking to be heard and to feel connected. Know that listening will help you feel connected. If you truly listen to another person, you are witnessing something sacred: a connection between two people. It's a miracle to be in these bodies with these abilities to talk, listen, understand, and respond. And each of us has his own language. Even if you speak to someone who speaks the same literal language, often the same words will land differently for different people. When listening to someone, truly listen.

FORGING THE PATH OF YOUR LIFE

Some say that creativity is linked to the Throat Chakra instead of the Sacral Chakra. Creativity at the Throat Chakra refers to the way you can contribute to the creation of your path in life based on your ability to express yourself. You create your life by being able to tell people your gifts and talents, by contributing to conversations, and by helping to solve problems. If you're standing on the sidelines because your Throat Chakra is weak, others may not notice you or realize how much you have to offer. Self-expression is key to your own development and to being able to use your talents in the world.

CONTRIBUTING TO EVOLUTION

When the Throat Chakra is balanced, you are able to stand in your truth. You are unafraid to communicate what you think, you listen to other people when they respond, and you are open to hearing other points of view. Together, you can solve problems, support each other, and enjoy life.

If your Throat Chakra is excessive, you might be overly talkative and self-righteous, causing another person to shut down. If your Throat Chakra is deficient, you will likely be soft-spoken and unable to stand up for what you need. The goal is to be an honest, effective communicator with a compassionate and authentic voice and ear.

THIRD EYE CHAKRA: SEEING BEYOND THE PHYSICAL

The Third Eye Chakra is your connection to the wisdom beyond your five physical senses. It's beyond your gut feelings that get input from outside stimuli; this is your connection to wisdom. This is the energetic center of your ability to telepathically send thoughts and images to others, including your animal friends.

WISDOM

Knowledge generated here is a different kind of knowing from what your mind or body know. This is your connection to wisdom of the ages. Here, messages come to you that you know to be true deep inside. When your Third Eye Chakra is balanced you are making choices that are aligned with who you truly are. You don't settle for less than what you deserve. What you deserve is kindness, respect, love, and all the support you need. For this chakra to truly be in balance, the other chakras must be too, which means that you'll be giving and receiving energy appropriately at the other levels.

In other words, your sense of what you truly deserve will be coming from a rational, grounded, compassionate, and mindful place. Then you will feel deep trust in the wisdom of the universe and make decisions from that place. You will trust that as you follow what you know to be true, with integrity and self-inquiry, you will be supported.

LOGIC

If you always make choices based solely on logic, then your Third Eye Chakra will not have much energy flowing through it. If you are not open to the possibility that something great can happen without you controlling every moment, without you figuring it all out first, then you will be limiting yourself to what you know or what you logically think is possible. There's so much out there that you might not yet know about. Can you be open to seeing what could unfold beyond your imagination?

With a balanced Third Eye Chakra, you will use your mind for all that it can give you. In this way, you will strengthen your knowledge with study and discernment. At the same time, you will be open to wisdom and gifts that can come to you when you step back, quiet the mind, and receive.

With this chakra, watch out for living in illusion. Illusion in this case could mean that you hold onto false beliefs about yourself and others, things you believe you've "sensed" without seeing if reality supports that belief. If you notice you hold on to certain judgments or beliefs that aren't serving your relationships, bring energy down from your Third Eye Chakra.

This chakra is where studies merge with intuition. When the Third Eye Chakra is functioning well, you are shining brightly in the world. You are confident that at this moment you are acting based on knowledge and your sense of what you know to be true. It might feel like you have to take some risks in life, and you will wisely decide in which ways a risk is worth it. With the grounding from the Root Chakra, the fluidity of the Sacral Chakra, the power of the Solar Plexus Chakra, the openness of the Heart Chakra, and the authenticity of the Throat Chakra, you are well equipped to handle what you decide to do.

NIGHTMARES AND OBSESSION

Because the Third Eye Chakra is a center for creativity and imagination, an excessive amount of energy in this area could cause nightmares and obsessions. Those are effects of an imagination in overdrive. If you notice you are prone to nightmares, or fantasies that become obsessions, then chakra healing practices to bring energy down from this chakra will help diffuse that energy.

CROWN CHAKRA: CONNECTING TO THE DIVINE

This is your connection to the blissful energy that you notice in the glory of a colorful sunset. Here is your connection to the energy of pure consciousness, the intelligence of the universe, the feeling that all is one. Having a well-balanced Crown Chakra helps strengthen your witness consciousness. You'll have an easier time not getting drawn into life's drama or attached to things you really don't need.

INNER PEACEFULNESS

When you have energy flowing freely through the Crown Chakra you have a sense of inner peace. You're not thinking about other people's opinions of you. You're not worried about your physical survival. You're not dreaming that things would be other than they are. Your personality is magnetic because you're fully alive. You are experiencing health mentally, physically, and spiritually. You have an understanding of boundaries so that you aren't oppressive, overbearing, or manipulative. You understand that you are a separate being in your body, needing to take care of your health and life, and you balance this with your understanding that we are all one.

EXHAUSTION

While exhaustion could use the help of all chakras, constant exhaustion and the inability to make decisions could indicate a deficient Crown Chakra. If you aren't connecting to the energy that exists beyond your physical body, if you feel limited to just what your own body and mind can produce, you may be prone to exhaustion.

PART 2

EXERCISES FOR BALANCING THE CHAKRAS

CHAPTER 5

BALANCING CHAKRAS WITH CRYSTALS, COLORS, AND REIKI

Crystals come from the earth and are believed to have certain healing qualities. When you place the crystals on your body, your intentions help the energy of the crystals enter into your body. The healing energy vibrates into your physical body and stimulates the chakras. The colors you choose can impact your experience as well. In this chapter, you'll also learn about the healing power that can flow from your hands—an art called Reiki.

CLEANSE
YOUR CRYSTALS

Before using your crystals, it's important to cleanse them of any negative energy they might be holding. You can cleanse them in several different ways:

* Leave them out overnight in the light of a full moon. The energy of the moon is said to clear them, returning them to their own pure vibration.
* Go to a fresh spring, and bathe your crystals with the points facing downward, toward the earth. (Before cleansing crystals in water, make sure your crystals aren't water soluble or else they will dissolve.)
* Create a salt solution using only sea salt and cool water in a glass container. Place the crystal in the solution, point down, and leave it to cleanse overnight. (Before cleansing crystals in water, make sure your crystals aren't water soluble or else they will dissolve.)
* Bury your crystal in a glass jar of dry sea salt, dried herbs, or outside in the earth overnight.
* "Smudge" your crystals by burning sage leaves and clearing the air around the crystals with the smoke from the burning sage. You can buy sage already bundled specifically for smudging, and one bundle can be used several times.

As you cleanse your crystals, imagine white light flooding through them. Send them love from your heart and fill them with an intention, such as, "I intend for this crystal to cultivate easeful healing for my highest good." It's always best to use the word "ease" and "easefully" when you set intentions for healing.

CHOOSE CRYSTALS FOR EACH CHAKRA
BASED ON THEIR COLOR

Books and charts differ about which crystals will help heal each chakra. You can cultivate your own relationship to crystals, and find which ones you can connect with. In the meantime, here are some standards that follow the rainbow as a guide:

Crystal	Color	Chakra
Bloodstone	Red	Root
Carnelian	Orange	Sacral
Citrine	Yellow	Solar Plexus
Jade or rose quartz	Green or pink	Heart
Lapis lazuli or turquoise	Blue	Throat
Amethyst	Indigo	Third Eye
Clear quartz or moonstone	White/clear or amethyst	Crown

The colors of the rainbow associated with each chakra will help bolster a deficient chakra. If you have an excessive chakra, rather than using a crystal to enhance that chakra, try using a crystal at the chakras below or above the excessive one to help diffuse the excess energy.

Connecting Your Intention to Crystals

Crystal healing potential is activated by the mind's intention. Just like all else on earth, crystals vibrate at certain frequencies. When placed near the chakra you want to balance, with your or your healer's intention, the crystal increases the healing vibration. Crystals amplify the energy you send through them and draw out negative energies from the body.

LEARN WHERE TO PLACE YOUR CRYSTALS WHEN YOU MEDITATE

One of the ways to use crystals for healing is to place one in your nondominant hand. Meditate on the crystal, its healing power, and the intention you want to infuse in it. Hold the crystal in your hand, and then move your hand toward the area of your body for healing to occur. Hold it there, with the crystal against your body, and meditate on its healing energy. On each exhale, envision the crystal drawing negative energy out. On each inhale, imagine the body absorbing the crystal's healing energy. (You can also use one of the meditations from Chapter 8 that is appropriate to that chakra.)

If you want to do this lying down, you can lay the crystals on your body and meditate with them there while you lie down. Some say that the less you touch the crystals the better, that way their energy remains purely their own. Others say as long as you keep your energy positive and on your healing, then your own hands and energy will enhance the crystal's effects. Try it both ways and see which way works best for you.

Be Patient

After you've finished using the crystals for this visualization, take some time for the healing effects to integrate. Give yourself a few moments, at least, before resuming other activities. Allow the healing influence of the crystals to sink in.

CREATE
A CRYSTAL ESSENCE

Try using your crystals to complement your chakra healing in yet another way by making an "essence" with quartz. Water will copy the crystal's vibration. To create an essence, place spring water in a glass container, and have crystals surrounding it with the points facing the water. After a few hours, pour it into your bath water or sip it a few times per day. It will last two to three days.

Essences, or elixirs, carry the vibrational quality of the crystal. To preserve your essence for more than a couple of days, place it in a dark glass bottle and add the same amount of vodka as liquid, as a preservative. Keep the bottle out of sunlight and out of contact with other bottles.

PRACTICE COLOR THERAPY
VIA YOUR WARDROBE

Working with a similar principle as crystal healing, color therapy uses the vibrational quality of color to resonate with your chakras. You can use the color associated with a particular chakra to add energy to the deficient chakras. Color therapy is used in various ways today. It comes from ancient wisdom and modern exploration and investigation. If you decide to use color therapy and want to deepen your knowledge, see the work of Theophilus Gimbel.

One way to increase the energy of a particular chakra is to wear the color of that chakra. For example, if you have a meeting in the afternoon and you want to increase your willpower, your self-esteem, and your fire, wear something yellow—the color associated with the Solar Plexus Chakra. In the chakras where you feel weak, do you notice a lack of that color in your life: in your wardrobe, room, or jewelry?

PRACTICE COLOR THERAPY
VIA THE NATURAL WORLD

Notice the myriad ways in nature that color appears, and use the vibration of the light from those natural objects to affect you. For example:

* For nourishing your heart take a walk in the green, spring grass.
* For groundedness in the winter, buy yourself a red poinsettia.
* To heighten your connection to spirit, keep purple lavender by your bedside.

Take time to look at these objects, and be mindful of what you surround yourself with in your home and office. Your body perceives the vibrations, even if you aren't looking. There's never a lack of inspiration from nature when it comes to color. Flowers come in spectacular shapes and colors, and the colors of animals, plants, and the sky are innumerable. Taking in the vibrations of color will stimulate your body if you aren't completely energetically closing yourself off.

Third Eye Chakra and Lavender

The smell of lavender is known for its relaxing and soothing effects. It helps with depression, anxiety, and insomnia. What's more, lavender is a bluish-purple color that is often associated with the Third Eye Chakra. And this chakra is often linked with the pineal gland, where melatonin is produced to help induce relaxation for sleep.

PRACTICE COLOR THERAPY
VIA COLORED GLASS

Another way to perform color therapy on yourself is to pour pure spring water into a glass bottle that is the color you desire. Set the bottle in the sunlight so that the water absorbs the vibration of the color. Then, throughout the day, take sips of that water.

Because your body is about 70 percent water, you absorb the vibrations around you just as water does. When you drink water that has a particular vibrational frequency, your body will copy that vibrational frequency. If you are new to color therapy, start slowly with this practice.

VISUALIZE HEALING
COLORED LIGHT

Because colors, thoughts, and your body are energy, they all work together. When you visualize colors traveling to a chakra, the energy of your thoughts literally affects your energy centers. The energy of your thoughts can also affect your body and your mind. Close your eyes and take a few deep, nourishing breaths. You can lie down, stand, or sit upright. Then put your awareness on each chakra one at a time. While your awareness is at each level, breathe in and out a few times until you can envision the color of that chakra in that part of your body. Use the rainbow as your guide for color.

* At the Root Chakra, envision red.
* At the Sacral Chakra, envision orange.
* At the Solar Plexus Chakra, envision yellow.
* At the Heart Chakra, envision green.
* At the Throat Chakra, envision blue.
* At the Third Eye Chakra, envision indigo.
* At the Crown Chakra, envision white, violet, or gold.

Start at the Root Chakra. Take slow, deep breaths in and out, and with your imagination connect to the perineum where the energy center is located. After a few natural breaths, as you breathe this time, imagine inhaling red light into the Root Chakra. Hold your breath in for a few seconds, imagining the colored light sustained there. Exhale, let go. Do this three times, then move up to the Sacral Chakra, and repeat the exercise visualizing the color orange. Continue up the chakras to the third eye, following the same pattern. When you finish with the third eye visualization, let your breath flow naturally in and out. Imagine your Crown Chakra glowing white light that envelops your entire body and expands upward, connecting you to the wide expanse. After doing this for a few moments, release the visualization. Cross your arms in front of you, hugging yourself across your chest or waist.

Feel the parts of you that are connected to the earth, grounding into the earth. Bring your awareness back into your body. And when you feel complete, open your eyes.

RELIEVE ANXIETY WITH
COLOR-BASED CHAKRA HEALING

Bringing your focus to all your chakras will help calm your anxiety. This color-based meditation will relax your body from head to toe.

1. Start your visualization at the Root Chakra, and imagine the Root Chakra glowing bright red. Feel your sitting bones stable, supported by the earth. Inhale and exhale with your attention at the root.

2. Place your hands one on top of the other on your torso at the location of the Sacral Chakra. Notice how your own hands on your body are grounding, comforting. Hold your hands at the area where the Sacral Chakra blossoms, and imagine a bright orange color as you inhale and exhale.

3. Move your hands up to the Solar Plexus Chakra. Imagine the bright yellow glow of your third chakra. Continue this up your body at the Heart, Throat, and Third Eye Chakras.

4. Finally, place your hands on top of your head at the Crown Chakra. Through your hands, visualize calming, healing white light flooding your brain through this chakra. Visualize yourself relaxed. Release your hands. Take a moment; notice if there have been any changes in how you feel. Notice your breath, your level of physical tension, and your mind.

GET A PROFESSIONAL
REIKI TREATMENT

Reiki is a healing modality during which a trained practitioner, called a master or teacher, acts as a vessel to transmit the life-force energy to your body. Reiki can be performed on you when you are fully clothed. A master can also do Reiki for you from a distance. If you become trained in Reiki, you can use it to charge anything with positive energy, or to heal or cleanse the chakras.

When someone is trained as a Reiki master, she is given attunements, which attune her to the energy of the universe. During these attunements, energy moves up and down the chakras. First, the energy goes from the Crown down to the Root, and then back up again. It can bring life into lifeless chakras, bringing you new levels of awareness and sensitivity. Ask friends or your integrative doctor for recommendations for a reputable Reiki practitioner in your area.

CHAPTER 6

BALANCING CHAKRAS WITH YOGA

While doing the postures of yoga, you focus and control your breath. When you direct the breath, you direct prana, your life force. And, as you move through yoga postures, you are helping to loosen tension and create space for prana to flow more easily throughout the body. That is why certain yoga postures are ideal for chakra healing: they can help release blocks by helping create space for energy to flow in places that may have been obstructed. When you unblock energy flow, you create health.

UNDERSTAND THE CONNECTION BETWEEN ENERGY AND PHYSICAL REALITY

Physical disease starts with something foreign, unsupportive, and obtrusive to the healthy joyful natural state of the life-force energy in you. The negative imprint in the energy field sustains and grows with your own thoughts, feelings, emotions, choices, and actions. Your energy field also responds to other people's energy and to environmental factors that you're exposed to (such as allergens, pollutants, and bacteria). When you notice negative energy around you or within you, and you try to pretend it's not there, you resist it, or you add to it; that taxes you. Instead of supporting your health, negativity diminishes it. Your mind, body, and chakras work to try to get you back to equilibrium. Your natural state is equilibrium and health, so your body and mind try as they might to be in balance.

While working to compensate for the effects of the negative energy, your body may fail to perform its usual essential functions like proper digestion or hormone secretion that you need for immunity. In addition, the negative energetic imprint affects your physical body and can cause headaches, migraine, ulcers, tumors, and more. What once begins as energy becomes manifest in physical reality.

Practicing Compassionate Self-Care

If you become ill or develop a serious physical limitation or emergency, it's not your fault. It's part of the journey of life. When disease shows up, care for yourself. And if there is something you can do to try to prevent it from happening again, see it as a chance to grow and learn on a soul level.

PREPARE YOURSELF
TO PRACTICE YOGA

Before you begin practicing yoga postures and breathing, think about these tips:

* Practice patience and mindfulness when you come to yoga. The postures may seem a little more challenging than you think, and you may not be able to do as much as you hope, at first. Part of the practice for you is being okay with where you are now.
* Wear comfortable clothes. When trying on clothes for a very gentle yoga practice, you want to make sure that you can do easy twists, lie down, sit up, and bend forward comfortably. Practice with bare feet to prevent sliding, and wear layers of clothes so if you get warm, you can remove a layer.
* It's helpful to have a few props on hand to make the postures more effective: a yoga mat, a blanket, a strap or tie, a chair (to modify positions that are too difficult at first), and at least one cushion.
* Enhance your practice with books, DVDs, or online courses on the yoga and chakra topics that interest you. Continue to gain knowledge. If you hear of a yoga teacher in your area whom others recommend, try a class. Continue to expand your experience to find out what works for you.
* Be sure to warm up. Anytime you do anything physical, whether it's taking a walk outside or doing a physical yoga practice, you need to warm up the body. Be intentional about the healing benefits you are about to receive: take time to center yourself and transition from your other activities into this practice.

POSES TO CENTER YOURSELF
FOR CHAKRA HEALING

1. **Sukhasana (Easy Pose):** Sit in a comfortable, seated position with your legs crossed. Place a cushion or a folded blanket under your sitz bones (sitting bones); this helps you sit up tall in Easy Pose while maintaining the natural curves in your spine.

    Gently place your hands in your lap or on the cushion. Close your eyes. Relax your forehead, eyes, jaw, and tongue. Scan all the way down your body, relaxing each body part as you breathe in and out naturally. After scanning the body, simply watch the breath as it flows in and out. Allow the belly, ribs, and chest to expand in three dimensions as you inhale. As you exhale, allow the chest, ribs, and belly to relax. Continue for several breaths. Then return to the natural breath, and open your eyes.

Sukhasana (Easy Pose), with blanket for support.

2. **Seated twist:** Place your hands palms down on your thighs. Gently exhale as you round the spine so that the bottom of your pelvis tilts forward and the crown of your head comes forward. Then inhale as you smoothly arch the spine by tilting the top of your pelvis forward, pressing your chest forward, and carefully tilting your head back. Repeat this sequence gently three to four times. Come back to neutral. Raise both arms up overhead, pull your abdomen in, gently elongate the spine, and slowly twist your torso to the left. Lower your arms, placing your right hand on your left knee and your left hand down to the earth beside or behind you. Inhale and exhale in this position. Then inhale as you raise both arms up and repeat this twist by turning to the other side. Inhale and exhale while twisted to the other side. Gently return to center. Bring your hands into your lap. Close your eyes. Breathe naturally for a few breaths. Then repeat this twist twice on each side.

Seated twist, supported by a chair.

3. **Tadasana (Mountain Pose):** Come into a steady and stable standing posture. Stand with your feet hip-width distance apart. Feel the balls of your feet and the heels rooting into the earth. Engage the muscles in your thighs while keeping the knees slightly and softly bent. Stand with your pelvis in a neutral position. Place your hands on your hips, inhale and imagine growing taller in the spine. Exhale and gently roll your shoulders up and back. Gaze forward, with the top of your head parallel to the ceiling. Breathe naturally, and stand strong in Mountain Pose with your fingertips extending down toward the earth.

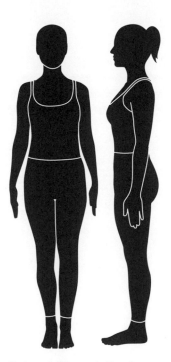

Tadasana (Mountain Pose).

4. **Standing side stretch:** Bring your right hand to your hip. On the inhale, raise the left arm out to the side and continue to raise it up in the air and overhead. On the exhale, lean slightly to the right side so that you create a slight arc in your torso. Inhale and exhale a few gentle breaths in this position. Gently inhale your left arm back up toward the center, bringing your whole torso into alignment. Exhale and release both arms to your sides. Repeat this on the other side. Pause and notice the effects.

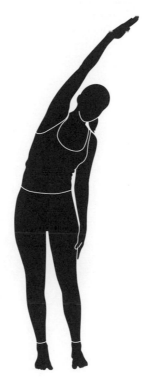

Standing side stretch.

5. **Light jumps:** Lightly jump several times in place, relaxing any part of you that doesn't need to be engaged as you jump. Let the arms hang. Let the tongue and jaw be relaxed. Keep breathing and jumping for three minutes, going at different paces. Jump and pause between jumps, then jump up and down without pausing. Open your mouth and let out a sound, "aaaahhhhhhhhhhh," as you do this—bouncing the tension out of the body, warming it up.

    Come to stillness. Notice if you feel any sensation as you stand still for a few breaths. Then look down at your feet and wiggle your toes. Add to your wiggling toes, wiggling fingers. Wiggle fingers and toes for a few breaths. Then pause. Observe how you feel.

6. **Ankle and wrist rotations:** Finally, rotate your ankles one at a time, in one direction then the other. Do this nine times for each ankle. Rotate your wrists nine times, then pause.

7. **Savasana (Corpse Pose):** Always end your practice with Savasana. Start by lying on your back with your legs straight on the floor. Place a cushion underneath your knees to help the low back relax. Allow your arms to relax along your sides. Slightly tilt your chin toward your chest, so the neck is long and relaxed. Relax your forehead, your eyes, your tongue, and your jaw. Let your whole body go, and lie in Savasana for several minutes.

Savasana (Corpse Pose).

When you are ready to get up, slowly roll to one side and press yourself up into a seated position. Notice how you feel. Then slowly transition into your day.

YOGA FOR THE
ROOT CHAKRA

1. **Prepare yourself:** Lie on your back on the floor. Relax. Feel yourself sinking into the support of the earth. Inhale, and on the exhale, bend your knees and draw them into your chest. Hold onto your calves or knees with your hands as you breathe in and out. Know that your colon is massaged as your belly presses into your thighs. Breathe in and out, noticing how the back of your body is supported by the earth and how this position brings attention into your physical body.

2. **Happy Baby Pose:** From here, come into Happy Baby Pose. Draw your knees apart and back toward your shoulders. Hold your right foot with your right hand and your left foot with your left hand, and lift your feet into the air with each knee bent at a 90-degree angle. The tops of your thighs are angled out from your torso, your knees are bent, and your feet are pointing toward the ceiling.

Happy Baby Pose.

Hold Happy Baby Pose and take seven slow, deep breaths. Visualize deep red energy coming up from the earth into your low back, which is solidly on the ground. Visualize the earth's energy swirling into your Root Chakra through your back. Rock your body side to side, if that feels soothing. Feel your back body grounding into the earth, and bring a gentle smile to your face. After several breaths, release this pose by hugging the legs into the chest, and roll over onto your right side in the fetal position. Relax in the fetal position, visualizing your Root Chakra as a glowing red lotus. Feel the support of the earth beneath you.

3. **Baddha Konasana (Bound Angle Pose):** Gently sit up. Feel your sitz bones against the earth, or put the cushion under your sitz bones if that's more comfortable. Come into Bound Angle Pose by bringing the soles of your feet together so that the knees are pointed outward, away from the body. If your thighs do not rest comfortably on or very near the earth, use blocks to support your thighs while you are seated on a cushion or a blanket.

Baddha Konasana (Bound Angle Pose).

4. **Hold your feet:** Now hold your feet in your hands. Breathe naturally as you gently massage your feet while in Bound Angle Pose. As you massage your feet be aware that you are touching acupressure points, sending prana throughout your body. And you are grounding yourself by bringing attention to your feet. After you've massaged your feet for a few moments, stop and hold your feet.

5. **Focus on your Root Chakra:** As you inhale and exhale a few times, send warmth and healing red energy from your hands to your feet and feel the glow rise up your legs to your Root Chakra. With a tall spine, inhale and pull in your abdomen to protect your spine. On the exhale, initiating the movement from the hips, gently lean forward, leading with the chest. Lean forward no more than 45 degrees. Hold this posture for a few deep breaths in and out.

6. **Release:** Release this posture by sitting up, releasing your hold on your feet, bending your knees up toward the chest, and slowly rolling yourself down onto your back. Do any small movements that your body is asking for as a countermovement to Bound Angle Pose.

YOGA FOR THE
SACRAL CHAKRA

1. **Prepare yourself:** Lie on your belly. Turn your head to one side, and take a few breaths. Enjoy the support of the earth.

2. **Warming up for Locust Pose:** Now begin warming up for Locust Pose. Place your arms down along your sides or fold your hands under your forehead. Place your forehead or chin on the floor. Inhale and press your pelvis into the earth. Pressing your pelvis into the earth, exhale and while keeping your pelvis grounded point the toes of your left foot toward the back of the room so that your left leg begins to lift off the floor. Press your pelvis into the earth, hold the left leg slightly off the floor as you inhale. Exhale, release the leg back down. Inhale, holding your pelvis to the floor. Exhale and point the toes of your right food toward the back of the room so that your right leg begins to lift off the floor. Press your pelvis into the earth, hold the right leg slightly off the floor as you inhale. Exhale, release the leg back down. Turn your head to one side, and take a few relaxing breaths.

Lifting one leg at a time, warming up for Locust Pose.

3. **Locust Pose:** Place your forehead or chin on the floor again. Pull your abdomen in, root your pelvis into the earth, and as you inhale, reach both feet toward the back of the room so that both legs are slightly off the ground.

As you breathe in and out, press your pelvis against the earth, hold your abdomen in, and gently raise your arms slightly off the ground with palms facing down while they stay next to your torso. Lift your chin off the ground to look forward and inhale and exhale a few times, holding Locust Pose. Imagine yourself gliding across the water, easily, smoothly, and gently. Envisioning your body gliding along the water energizes the Sacral Chakra, whose element is water. Pressing your pelvis into the earth also brings energy to the Sacral Chakra, which is located below the navel. Release this pose by bringing your legs and arms down, turning your head to the side, and taking a few breaths. Allow your body to take a moment to receive the benefits of the posture.

Locust Pose.

4. **Standing hip sways:** After you have released Locust Pose, take your time and gently come up to standing. If you want to, for this upcoming part, put on music that you enjoy—do these movements at the pace the music moves you. Stand with your legs wider than hip-distance apart. Place your hands on your hips, and breathe as you sway your hips side to side. After several breaths, pause.

5. **Standing pelvic sways:** Now sway your pelvis back and forth. Breathe as you repeat these movements several times.

6. **Standing hip circles:** Now make circles with your hips by putting those movements together, swaying to the right, to the front, to the left, and to the back. Do this smoothly and gently. Luxuriate in this fluid movement, for several breaths, then do it in the other direction.

7. **Fluid movement:** Now breathe naturally for a few moments and allow your body to move in any way that it feels it wants to. Make the movements fluid, like water, stimulating your Sacral Chakra. If your body doesn't feel the need for more movement, be still, and take note of any sensations in your body.

8. **Goddess Pose:** Come back to a neutral standing position, and leave the music on. Enter Goddess Pose. Place your hands on your hips. Stand with your feet more than hip-width distance apart. Pivot your feet so your toes are turned out, 45 degrees. Feel your feet rooted into the earth. Gently pull your abdomen in, inhale, and on the exhale sink your sitz bones downward with your spine tall as your knees bend and point away from each other. Keep your abdomen in, and lift your arms up to shoulder height. Bend your elbows 90 degrees and turn your palms to face you.

Goddess Pose.

Take seven deep breaths, feeling your belly expand and contract at the level of the Sacral Chakra. Ground yourself into the earth through your powerful legs. If your hips want to move a little bit, allow them some fluid, easy movement. Keep your legs strong, grounded.

9. **Release:** As you stand in Goddess Pose, you are glowing. Your chest expands as you shine your light, and your strong arms, abdomen, and legs ground you emotionally. Release this posture, straighten the legs and stand up, and relax the arms down by your side. Pause, and notice how you feel. A balanced Sacral Chakra allows you to feel you are allowed to enjoy life, with stability in the face of emotional challenges.

YOGA FOR THE
SOLAR PLEXUS CHAKRA

The Solar Plexus Chakra is about transformation, using your own fire to make things happen in your life with self-confidence, a positive outlook, appropriate action, and groundedness.

1. **Archer Pose:** To begin a sequence for the Solar Plexus Chakra, come into the Archer Pose, which exemplifies this energy. Come up with an intention for the next step in your life. Face forward, with your legs and feet together. Step your right foot approximately 2 feet in front of you. Feel stable. If you need to, place your foot a little further in front of you and a little to the right, for balance. Make it stable for your body; everyone is different. Inhale as you lift your right arm straight out in front of you at eye level. Make a fist with the fingers of your right hand and point your right thumb up to the ceiling. Bend your left arm and place your left hand on the back of your head. Inhale, pull your abdomen in, gently elongate the spine, and with a soft gaze on your right thumb, begin to twist your torso to the right. Keep your gaze on your thumb as you twist your torso, and your right arm naturally moves with the torso, toward the right side of the room. Keep your gaze on that right thumb, and continue to twist. You are looking over the edge of the arrow.

Archer Pose.

2. **Consider your intention:** When you come to your stopping point, hold this position and call to mind your intention. Gaze at the thumb, keep your abdomen in, and breathe in and out a few times, focusing on the thumb and your intention. See if you can slowly twist further. Pause. Then gently release this posture by unwinding your torso and releasing your arms down.

3. **Archer Pose (other side):** After pausing for a moment, do the Archer Pose on the other side. After you have completed Archer Pose on both sides, step your feet together, bring your hands to your solar plexus, and envision your Solar Plexus Chakra glowing like the yellow sun. As you twisted your torso in the Archer Pose, you brought energy to the center of your core. This helps wring out energy blockages there, and fills your intention with motivational energy.

YOGA FOR
THE HEART CHAKRA

1. **Fish Pose:** Lower yourself down onto your back for Fish Pose. Lie down with your legs straight out along the floor and your arms by your sides. Slide your hands toward each other, placing one hand underneath each buttock. Engage your abdomen muscles, and when you inhale press your forearms down and slowly lift your waist off the floor, creating an arch in your thoracic spine, the section of the spine behind your heart. Exhale, press your sitz bones and forearms into the earth. Inhale, expand your chest and bring the back of your head to the floor, chin toward the ceiling. Keep most of your weight on the forearms and on the sitz bones and legs as they press into the floor.

Fish Pose.

2. **Focus on your Heart Chakra:** Inhale and exhale a few times, feeling the energy come to the Heart Chakra. To release from the Fish Pose, exhale as you press through the forearms and sitz bones, and gently take the weight off of your head. Bring your torso back down to the ground, and gently place the back of your head on the floor. Pause and notice the effects. Make any slight movements that your body calls for in response to the Fish Pose.

YOGA FOR
THE THROAT CHAKRA

1. **Table Pose:** Come into Table Pose, on all fours, on your hands and knees. In this position, do three rounds of Lion's Breath. To do this, face forward. Inhale, and give a forceful, long exhale as you open your mouth, stick your tongue out and down, and roll your eyes upward. When you've run out of air, release your facial expression to normal. Then inhale, and do Lion's Breath again.

Table Pose.

2. **Sit cross-legged:** Gently sit back into a simple cross-legged position with your hands in your lap. Use the cushion under your sitz bones, and if your knees are higher than your hips, place cushions or blocks under your thighs to support them. Gently drop your chin down to your chest, and breathe seven deep breaths in this position.

3. **Tilt head to the right:** Inhale, and on the exhale gently roll your head to the right so that your right ear is near your right shoulder. Inhale and exhale a few times in this position.

4. **Tilt head to the left:** On an exhale gently roll your chin back toward the center of your chest, and then over to the left. Inhale and exhale a few times in this position. Bring your head back up into a neutral position. Pause.

5. **Shell Mudra:** While looking in front of you do the Shell Mudra. Hold your left hand so that the fingers are pointing toward the sky and facing to the right. With the fingers of your right hand, hold your left thumb. As you do this, touch the left middle finger with your right thumb. Hold this Shell Mudra in front of your chest. Inhale and exhale seven times. Chant *ham* (a "seed" mantra for this chakra) on the exhale each time. This will help strengthen the Throat Chakra.

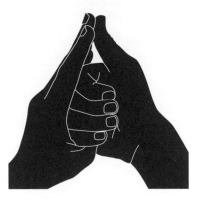

The Shell Mudra.

YOGA FOR
THE THIRD EYE CHAKRA

1. **Savasana:** Gently lie down on your back with your legs straight on the floor. Get in a comfortable position for Savasana, or Corpse Pose. You may want to have a cushion underneath your knees to help your low back relax. Also, you may want a blanket over your body to keep you warm.

Savasana (Corpse Pose).

2. **Prana:** Once you are in the position for Corpse Pose, rub your hands together vigorously to create warmth, prana. Cover your eyes with the cupped palms of your hands. Feel the prana balancing out the energy of the eyes, behind the eyes, and in the mind. Repeat this palming of your eyes three times. Take deep, nourishing breaths as you do it. Then release your hands. Relax.

3. **Visualize:** Now visualize a deep indigo color swirling in the area of the third eye. Hold this visualization for a few breaths. Then notice if your imagination sees anything else: colors, animals, landscapes. Allow your imagination to travel for a few moments. Notice if any symbols or messages come to you.

YOGA FOR
THE CROWN CHAKRA

1. **Savasana:** In Savasana, or Corpse Pose (see previous exercise), use your fingertips to gently massage your head. Make sure you massage the top of your head, gently bringing energy to the crown. Massage your entire scalp. Then bring your arms down by your sides, and sink into relaxation pose. Let go. Open up to the energy of the universe. There's nothing for you to do in this pose but let go. If you fall asleep, that's okay too.

Savasana (Corpse Pose).

2. **Sit up and visualize:** After you have stayed in Savasana for seven to ten minutes, or longer if you have time, gently roll over to your right side in fetal position. Then gently sit up. Take a moment to envision each chakra glowing with its associated color. Bring your hands into prayer position at your Heart Chakra, and offer appreciation for the energy that has moved through you.

PERFORM THE
SIX MOVEMENTS OF THE SPINE

You can move your spine in six different ways. When you practice slowly doing the six movements of the spine, you are warming up the spine and allowing the free flow of life-force energy through the chakras. After you have been still for a long time, for example after sleeping the whole night through, your spine could use a warm-up before you start your day.

1. **Cat and Cow Poses:** Two movements of the spine can be done with the Cat and Cow Poses. To do the spinal movements, come onto your hands and knees. For Cat Pose, exhale, and round your back so that your belly button rises up toward the spine, your tailbone tilts downward, and your head comes down between your arms.

Cat Pose.

On the inhale, come into Cow Pose. Arch your back so that your belly dips toward the floor, your shoulder blades come toward each other, your eyes look forward, and your tailbone lifts. Switch back and forth between the poses three times, coordinating them with the inhale and exhale.

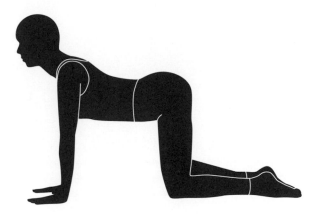

Cow Pose.

2. **Lateral Angle Pose:** Two of the movements of the spine create a sideways C curve of the spine. Sit in a comfortable position with your legs crossed on the floor. Alternatively, stack two blocks on top of each other, and sit on top of them with your legs crossed in front of you, or have your legs bent underneath you in a kneeling position. Place your left hand on your left hip. Inhale and lift your right arm straight up, then exhale and gently lean to the left. Pause. Inhale, and come back to center. Gently place your hands on your thighs, and pause. Place your right hand on your right hip. Inhale and lift your left arm straight up. Exhale, and gently lean to the right. Inhale back to center.

Lateral Angle Pose.

3. **Twisting:** The last two movements of the spine can be performed by a gentle twist. Before you twist, it's important to first elongate. To do this, inhale and imagine that there is a string from the top of your head to the ceiling, and it's pulling you up slowly against the pull of gravity. Always do this before entering into a twist when you are standing or sitting. To enter into a lying-down twist, lie down on your back with your knees bent so that your feet are flat on the floor. Extend your arms out to the sides at 90-degree angles from your torso, so you are in a T position. Inhale, and on the exhale let your knees drop to the left. Inhale back to center. Exhale, and let your knees drop to the right. Inhale back to center. Do this a few more times, and if it's comfortable for you, then turn your head in the opposite direction of your knees each time. Don't forget to inhale and exhale with each movement.

Lying-down twist.

Visualize Prana in Your Spine

With every inhale and exhale, imagine prana flowing into your spine and the areas of your body that are opening up as a result of the six movements. Notice how it feels first thing in the morning to give your spine these ten or fifteen minutes of attention.

GET PERSPECTIVE WITH
A YOGA MEDITATION

The following exercise can help you step into the right side of your brain when you are used to spending a lot of time doing left brain–centered activities. Find a spot where you are out of the range of anything work-related. Be out of sight and energetic range of electronic devices and cluttered shelves. Find a place where there is free space in front of a wall, or where you can bring a chair for one of the physical postures you will be doing. This sequence will help you see things from a new perspective.

1. **Prepare yourself:** Find a spot where there is wall space, or have a chair handy. Sit comfortably, close your eyes, and relax. Let out a sigh of relief: inhale, and exhale with a sound. Sigh a few times, relaxing the lines in the forehead, relaxing the jaw, relaxing the shoulders.

2. **Legs Up the Wall Pose:** Now position yourself in Legs Up the Wall Pose, in which you will lean your legs up against the wall or a chair. First sit sideways on the floor so that your right side is facing the wall or chair. Sit so that your right hip is approximately 1 foot away from the wall or the chair. If you are new to this pose or not too flexible, start further away, and explore the next two steps at different distances to see what feels comfortable. This is not a contest: what feels good for your body is healthiest. Also, it may be more comfortable to put a bolster or folded blanket close to the wall or chair to support your low back.

Supported Legs Up the Wall Pose.

3. **Raise your legs:** Lean over to your left onto your left forearm while you begin to gently raise your legs up and to the right. As you do this, pivot your body so that you end up on your back with both legs leaning up against the wall. If you are using a chair, remain on the floor, and raise your legs up onto the seat of the chair. Using the chair, have thighs at a 90-degree angle in relationship to your lying-down torso, and your knees bent so your thighs and calves create a 90-degree angle. Your calves rest on the seat of the chair.

4. **Relax:** With your legs up the wall, your legs can be at an angle. The point is for your legs to be up, and for you to feel no strain. Now let your entire body relax, with your legs up the wall or on

the chair. Feel your back body sink into the floor: head, shoulder blades, back, and buttocks release into the support of the earth.

5. **Adjust your perspective:** As you lie here, with your legs up the wall or on the chair, open your eyes for a moment and look at your feet. This is a different perspective from how you are most of the day. Normally, your feet are beneath your head, now they are higher than your head. Acknowledge that your feet now have time to rest from the physical weight they carry. Notice that gravity is working on your legs in a different way. Down is now up, up is now down: different perspective.

6. **Breathe:** Take several deep breaths, with a longer exhale than inhale. Relax.

7. **Activate your prana:** Palm your eyes by rubbing your hands together vigorously to create warmth, prana. Once you've generated heat, close your eyes and carefully place the cupped palms of your hands over your eyes. Breathe in the prana and warmth. As you do this, prana comes into the upper part of your body, including the upper chakras.

8. **Visualize your Throat Chakra glowing blue:** Keep your palms here. Breathe and relax. Envision your Throat Chakra a glowing, azure blue. Breathe a few breaths with this visualization.

9. **Visualize a lotus at your Third Eye Chakra:** Envision your Third Eye Chakra as a lotus, glowing a deep midnight-sky indigo. Breathe a few times with this visualization of the indigo lotus at your third eye.

10. **Visualize a sphere coming from your Crown Chakra:** Now envision your Crown Chakra projecting a brass-colored golden sphere above your head in the shape of a globe-like sun. It shines with a mirroring quality.

11. **Charge your Solar Plexus Chakra:** Reach your hands above your crown, and grasp that solid ball of gold, that energy that

you've just imagined into being with your thoughts. Carry that ball of energy from above your head to above your solar plexus, and allow the energy to charge your Solar Plexus Chakra. Hold your hands over that spot, nourishing the Solar Plexus Chakra. Breathe a few times.

12. **Release:** To release this posture, spread your hands and arms wide, let the ball of energy go. Slowly bend your knees into your chest. Roll over onto your right side. When you are ready, sit up. Slowly move on to whatever activity you have planned next.

This exercise helps you begin to see things from a new perspective while lying with your legs up the wall or on a chair. While you do this, the visualization strengthens your Throat, Third Eye, and Crown Chakras, before you bring that universal energy into your Solar Plexus Chakra. With a stronger Solar Plexus Chakra, you have self-confidence and will to create something new.

IMPROVE DIGESTION WITH YOGA

Digestive disturbances like constipation are all too common and can be related to imbalances in the Solar Plexus Chakra. If you become constipated, try to relax and allow your digestive system to work. Drink warm water. Ask your doctor if the herbal remedy triphala might also help your bowels move. Other natural remedies include eating prunes, taking a relaxing walk, and trying this Wind-Relieving Pose:

1. **Prepare yourself:** Lie on your back with your legs straight out on the floor. Take a few deep breaths, relax into the support of the earth.
2. **Wind-Relieving Pose:** Bend your right knee and draw it up to your chest as far as is comfortable. Keep the left leg straight on the ground. Use both hands to hold the right knee into your chest. Breathe deeply several times, feeling your belly rise up against your right thigh. On an exhale, straighten the right leg back onto the floor. Repeat these motions, using the left leg. Gently roll over onto your left side. Then slowly get up.

Wind-Relieving Pose.

You start this exercise on the right side and then move to the left because that follows the direction of digestion in your colon. Your colon ascends up the right side, then descends on the left. You're physically helping it along with this exercise, and you're relaxing.

Eat Mindfully

To help keep your digestion strong and good, be mindful when you eat. Choose foods carefully according to what your body needs. And when you eat, sit down. First look at your food and take a moment before diving in. Spend a moment being thankful for what you have. Even take a moment to smell the food. This helps your digestive process begin. And when you're finished, sit for a moment before rushing off to the next task.

CHAPTER 7

BALANCING CHAKRAS WITH PRANAYAMA (BREATH WORK)

Pranayama is the practice of noticing, controlling, and using the breath to help guide prana through the body. Breathing techniques help balance the chakras and can be used in various everyday situations to calm you down, energize you, or cheer you up. Visualization is an integral part of pranayama. Depending on the specific pranayama that you choose to do, you will coordinate your breath with visualizations of where you want the breath and healing energy to travel. Pranayama is an ancient practice with many benefits for modern life. And perhaps the best part is that it's free and always available. You don't have to buy any materials to do it, and you can practice it wherever you are.

UNDERSTAND
PRANAYAMA

Pranayama is one of the eight limbs of yoga, and it consists of various techniques of inhaling, retaining, and exhaling your breath. The word *pranayama* can be broken into its two parts: *prana*, "life force," and *yama*, "to restrain" or "hold back."

Pranayama exercises vary in their difficulty, intensity, and purpose. For some you add the movement of arms and legs; for others you sit still and quietly. Some involve making sound. As with any practice, start slow or with only a few repetitions to allow your body to become acclimated. Over time, you can increase repetitions and level of difficulty.

Visualization is an important part of pranayama. Depending on the specific pranayama that you choose to do, you will coordinate your breath with visualizations of where you want the breath and healing energy to travel. You have at your disposal a free and invaluable self-healing tool: you can direct healing energy to wherever you feel pain or discomfort in the body. And you can use it to help calm your overactive mind too. Sometimes the hardest part is just to remember to do it. Visualizations strengthen the Third Eye Chakra, in particular, whose energy connects you to imagination and seeing areas of yourself and existence that the biology of the eye cannot.

Pranayama is an important addition to yoga practice. Whether you use Dirgha to keep the breath steady or Kapalabhati at times to increase energy, pranayama helps keep the mind steady. Here are guidelines for how to match up chakras with pranayama:

Chakras and Pranayama		
Chakras	**Pranayama**	**Effect**
Root and Sacral	Dirgha	Grounding
Solar Plexus	Kapalabhati	Stimulating
Heart	Dirgha with Ujjayi	Soothing
Throat	Dirgha with Ujjayi	Stimulating
Third Eye	Nadi Shodhana	Balancing
	Anuloma Viloma	

CHECK IN WITH EACH CHAKRA
USING DIRGHA BREATH

Pronounced "deer-gha," Dirgha is also called the yogic breath. It's a breath you can use throughout your yoga practice and life. It's deep breathing, focusing on expanding the torso to allow as much breath as possible to fill the lungs. The purpose of this breath is to focus your attention to bring your awareness to the present moment. It's a perfect way to become present for meditation or the physical yoga postures, to separate this moment from the business of your day. You can also do it first thing in the morning, each day, to transition from whatever you experienced in sleep to a new place from which to start your day.

Practicing Dirgha breath can support you throughout your day. It's a pranayama you can do without drawing attention to yourself. Whether you're at work, standing in line, or taking a walk, you can practice this deep breathing technique to bring more vitality and a sense of calm to your life. And the more often you practice, the more it will become second nature in times of stress.

Dirgha Pranayama Practice

1. Sit or lie down in a comfortable position, with your spine supported.
2. Close your eyes or fix your gaze softly on a still object.
3. Inhale, expanding the belly area in three dimensions. Envision the breath going deep into the belly. As you do this, imagine that lower part of your entire torso expanding in three dimensions—the side and back body, as well as the front.
4. Keep inhaling, and imagine the torso expanding at the level of the rib cage.

5. Continue to inhale, expanding the chest in front and behind to the shoulder blades.
6. Finally, as you exhale, allow the chest, rib cage, then belly to soften.

Dirgha pranayama is a deep, long inhale and slow exhale. You can repeat it several times. The inhale physically starts in the area of the Sacral Chakra and physically continues up to the Throat Chakra, though you can envision it going up to your Third Eye Chakra. To practice chakra visualization with Dirgha, as you inhale and expand the belly, envision the breath traveling down to feed the lotus at the Root Chakra. As you continue to expand the torso on the inhale, envision the location of each chakra along the way, up to the Third Eye Chakra. To keep your awareness on the calming effects of being in your physical body, do not envision the breath going up to the Crown Chakra. Keep the visualizations between the Root Chakra and the Third Eye Chakra for embodiment.

Dirgha for Low Back Pain

Dirgha can help with low back pain. Sit or lie down with a rolled-up towel placed comfortably in the natural curve of your spine. If you lie down, also try placing a pillow underneath your knees. As you inhale deeply, envision breath traveling with healing energy to the place where your back hurts. Exhale, let go, and relax. Repeat.

FIND PEACE WITH UJJAYI,
THE CALMING OCEAN SOUND

To practice Ujjayi pranayama, you slightly constrict the back of your throat as you breathe in and out. This will cause a sound that will resonate in your ears like the tides of the ocean as they go out to sea and come back to land, spilling across the sand. Ujjayi is a calming breath, and the sound is another tool to help you focus the mind.

To practice it, breathe in and out, in Dirgha (see instructions in Check In with Each Chakra Using Dirgha Breath). Add this sound to each inhale and exhale. A helpful tip: Ujjayi is also described as sounding like Darth Vader, the character from the Star Wars films.

BALANCE YOURSELF WITH
NADI SHODHANA BREATH

Nadi Shodhana is known as the channel-purifying breath. When you alternate the flow of breath from one side to the other, you are balancing and purifying the flow of energy through the ida and pingala nadis (remember that nadis are the major lines of energy in the body), as well as the flow to alternate sides of the brain.

Why is it important to balance energy in both sides of your brain? Each side of the brain is associated with certain functions. The right side is connected to creative and intuitive functioning, and the left side is associated with logical and rational thought. When you alternate the flow of energy from one side to the other, you are balancing them so that one isn't feeling quite as dominant over the other. This kind of breathing has a balancing and calming effect on your entire system.

Nadi Shodhana is a great way to switch gears. If you are transitioning from a hectic schedule to your yoga practice, Nadi Shodhana is a great way to transition. Nadi Shodhana is also a great breath to use when you are making decisions. Because many people form habits of making decisions using one of the hemispheres of the brain, by using Nadi Shodhana first you can make decisions from a more balanced mind-set. You will be using both your logical and intuitive faculties as you consider the choices.

Nadi Shodhana Practice

1. Find a comfortable seated position. Make sure your spine is upright, no slouching.
2. Do a few moments of Dirgha to center yourself (see instructions in Check In with Each Chakra Using Dirgha Breath).

3. Hold your hand in Vishnu Mudra. (To do this, keep your thumb, ring finger, and pinky extended, while your pointer and middle fingers are bent down toward your palm.)
4. With eyes closed use your right thumb to close your right nostril. Exhale through your left nostril.
5. With your right thumb still holding your right nostril closed, inhale through the left nostril.
6. Use the ring finger of your right hand to close your left nostril.
7. Exhale through the right nostril.
8. Inhale through the right nostril. And, repeat the process from step 4.

As you practice rounds of Nadi Shodhana, begin to extend the length of the inhale and the exhale. Do this comfortably to induce relaxation and to balance the hemispheres of the brain. When you've completed the rounds you want to do, take several moments to be still and notice the effects of the practice.

Nadi Shodhana to Alleviate Menopause Symptoms

Nadi Shodhana is said to help with the symptoms of menopause. Symptoms such as hot flashes, difficulty sleeping, and mood swings can be tempered with Nadi Shodhana because it's designed to help create balance. Practicing for ten to fifteen minutes at a time once or twice a day could alleviate menopausal symptoms.

FOCUS WITH
ANULOMA VILOMA BREATH

Anuloma Viloma is alternate nostril breathing. It is similar to Nadi Shodhana because you alternate nostrils, and the addition for Anuloma Viloma is that you practice retention. In the retention there is time to notice and direct energy while increasing inward focus.

Anuloma Viloma Practice

1. Sit in a comfortable seated position.
2. Practice Nadi Shodhana for a few rounds (see instructions in Balance Yourself with Nadi Shodhana Breath).
3. To start Anuloma Viloma, retain the breath between the inhale and the exhale.
4. As you get more comfortable, hold the breath longer between the inhale and the exhale, and just observe what happens in your body.
5. Repeat the cycles of Anuloma Viloma for up to fifteen minutes to receive balancing benefits of the practice. Then, after you are finished, pause and notice the effects.

After doing this or any of the other breathing exercises, pause and notice. Allow the body to adjust from the pranayama back to normal breathing. When you do this, you also allow the effects to sink in. Keep the breathing practices meditative. Do not strain.

ENERGIZE YOURSELF
WITH KAPALABHATI BREATH

Kapalabhati stokes your inner fire. It's a way of raising your energy. You can do Kapalabhati breathing if you're feeling sluggish and need a boost. You can also do it during your yoga poses to add more fire to your practice. It's best to wait to do Kapalabhati for two hours after a light meal or four hours after a heavy meal.

Kapalabhati is primarily associated with the Solar Plexus Chakra. When you do this breathing exercise, you engage muscles in the area of the solar plexus with a forceful exhale, then you allow the air to flow in on a passive inhale. The Solar Plexus Chakra is strengthened with the increase in movement, energy, and heat.

Another great time to practice Kapalabhati is when you are watching a show or movie. Watching TV can be a sluggish experience, and you could sit there for hours and hours in the same position. During breaks, sit or stand up and practice Kapalabhati. It's a great way to engage your internal fire and get energy flowing at a time when you are otherwise sedentary.

Kapalabhati works well as a break from sitting at the computer too. Take breaks for this pranayama to energize yourself and boost your metabolism. It's a perfect addition to any lifestyle that calls for extended amounts of sitting still and staring at a computer screen.

Kapalabhati Practice

1. Get into a comfortable seated or standing position.
2. Practice a few rounds of Dirgha breath (see instructions in Check In with Each Chakra Using Dirgha Breath).
3. Inhale deeply.

4. Forcefully contract the abdomen muscles toward the spine, swiftly pushing the air out.
5. Relax the muscles, passively allowing the air to rush back into your body.
6. Repeat at a moderate pace, forcefully pressing air out, passively allowing it back in.
7. As you become experienced, you can do this in rapid succession.
8. After fifteen rapid contractions of your abdomen and passive inhalations, allow a long inhale and exhale. Relax while your breath returns to normal.
9. Repeat fifteen rounds three times, if your body will allow it. Increase the repetitions to thirty per round when you are comfortable and used to Kapalabhati.

Before practicing Kapalabhati and all of the breathing exercises, be sure that your nasal passages are clear. Have some tissues nearby, just in case. And it's best not to practice pranayama if you have a cold or upper respiratory infection.

To restore the chakras with pranayama, combine Dirgha breath with visualization to send the breath where you want it to go. To assist your visualization, place a hand on the body part you want to heal. Breathe deeply and envision the breath traveling to where your hand is placed. At the same time, imagine healing energy emanating from your hand to that spot.

Before You Practice Kapalabhati

Kapalabhati is not recommended for women who are pregnant or for people with uncontrolled high blood pressure. It is also not intended for people who have recently had surgery, especially anywhere in the torso. You can control how vigorously you do the practice, so always be mindful of how your body handles the movement and flow of air.

CLEAR UP ACNE
WITH DIRGHA BREATH

There are several ways to address acne using chakra healing. First, you can infuse spring water with the energy of blue light, which is cooling, and sip the water a few times during the day. Second, here's an example of a breathing sequence and visualization that can help with acne:

1. Sit upright in a comfortable position, with your hands resting in your lap.
2. Notice several breaths flow in and out.
3. Begin Dirgha breath (see instructions in Check In with Each Chakra Using Dirgha Breath) and imagine blue light filling your torso as it expands with the breath: first in the belly, then the ribs, then the chest, and up into the third eye. As the blue light travels up your torso imagine it passing through each chakra, from the root to the third eye, bringing cooling energy to all the chakras. Exhale it out. Repeat this visualization several times.
4. Continue deep breathing. Change your visualization to the image of your skin clearing. Imagine how it looks clearing up and then all clear. As you breathe in and out several times focus on the image of your clearing and clear skin.

Staying emotionally balanced and calm helps cure acne. Throughout the day, notice if you are carrying tension in your face. Bring your internal awareness to your face; notice if your jaw is relaxed. Create space between the top and bottom rows of the back teeth to help relax the jaw. Use your fingers to gently massage in circular motions the spot where the top jawbone connects to the lower. Next, bring the fingertips of the first two fingers of each hand together at the third eye. Inhale, and as you exhale draw the fingertips away from each other across your forehead—from the third eye to the temple on each side. Do this a few times. Close your eyes, inhale and exhale a few times imagining your face relaxed, clear, and healthy.

Positive Visualizations

As often as possible when you think of your skin, imagine it cooling down and clearing up. Do not focus negative attention and frustration on how you look. This will continue to aggravate your emotions, which counteracts the healing work you're doing. The negative visuals and emotions cancel out the positive ones.

CHAPTER 8

BALANCING CHAKRAS WITH MEDITATION

Meditating is one of the main ways to heal your chakras. All you'll do is observe your mind and learn to focus on an image, color, sound, your breath—or nothing at all. If you haven't intentionally meditated before, you might think, "I can't meditate." Let that thought go. That's your first lesson in meditation: let the thought drift by. In meditation the goal is always the same: as the potentially distracting thoughts come up, let them go by. A common metaphor is: your thoughts are clouds drifting across the sky.

TRUST THAT YOU
CAN MEDITATE

Meditation can be the most wonderful experience of your life because it's when you experience life right here, right now. You will allow your attention to be on the quiet and basic goodness of the present moment. Worries about the past, present, or future are not your concern when you meditate. You may have the idea that to meditate, you must sit in a particular position on the floor, with your legs crossed, and do something to attain a state of bliss and enlightenment. Fortunately, meditation isn't about these things. You are meditating when you don't get caught up in doing, planning, judging, and worrying. Meditating is when you can just be. Here are some ways to prepare yourself for a meditation session:

* **Create a silent space:** Make sure that you've turned your ringer off. Go to a place in your house where you can close a door and not be bothered. If there are others in your home, let them know you'd like not to be disturbed for the amount of time you've set aside. Sometimes it's easiest to do it first thing in the morning, or before going to bed.

* **Find a seat:** Once you are ready, find a comfortable, seated position. You can sit on the floor with your legs crossed and a cushion underneath your tailbone. Another option is to sit upright in a chair with your legs uncrossed. If, when you sit in the chair, your feet do not touch the floor, rest them on cushions, a hassock, or anything that is comfortable for your feet to rest on.

* **Stay warm:** Make sure you will be warm enough. Wrap a blanket around your shoulders to stay warm.

* **Check your posture:** Gently sit up straight. Don't strain, but do keep the curve in your lumbar spine. Bring your chin down

slightly so that the top of your head is parallel to the ceiling: this allows the top of your spine, the cervical vertebrae, to rest in a neutral position. Inhale and shrug your shoulders up, and on the exhale gently roll them back and down. Resume normal breathing, and allow your arms to hang with your hands in your lap or on your thighs. Your palms can be open in the "receiving" position, or faced down in the "introspective" position.

* **Focus on your breath:** Notice if there's any tension in your jaw. Allow your teeth to part slightly at the back of the mouth to help release tension. Gently close your eyes, and notice the breath go in and out. Just notice the breath without controlling it. As distracting thoughts come to mind, acknowledge them as thoughts, and return your focus to the breath. Notice how your body expands on the inhale, contracts on the exhale. And, again, each time a thought comes up, acknowledge it, and if it helps to think the word "thinking" to label it, do that. Then let it pass. Voilà! You are meditating. Do not try to stop the thoughts from coming. Instead, allow whatever comes up to come up, and then allow it to drift by without hanging on or fueling that thought by engaging with it.

Some days meditating might be easier than other days. That's okay too—just accept it without judgment.

CONDUCT A
BODY SCAN MEDITATION

A body scan meditation allows you to sit or lie down and place your attention on one body part at a time. Then you'll relax that body part by inhaling and exhaling, imagining the breath traveling to that area. The body scan is a way to become present to your body and to feel grounded. It helps you recognize that the ground literally supports you, and you can let go and release. The practice is also good for tuning in to how you are, which becomes so important to chakra healing since deficiencies or excesses in the chakras manifest in the physical body. Here's an example of a body scan:

1. Lie down on your back, with your legs outstretched comfortably on the floor. Place a pillow or cushion underneath your knees. Do not put a pillow underneath your head. Cover yourself with a blanket if you think you might get cold, as your body temperature will drop as you relax deeply.

2. Take a slow, deep inhale through your nose and exhale through your mouth. Let go. Feel yourself supported by the ground, by Mother Earth. You are held, you can let go. Pay attention to your breath flowing in and out for a few breaths.

3. Turn your attention to your right foot. Notice your toes, relax the entire foot. Relax the right ankle. Feel your entire right leg. Relax the right leg. Notice the right side of your torso. Relax the right side of your torso. Relax the right shoulder. Relax the top of the right arm, relax the forearm. Relax the right hand, including the right fingers. Relax the entire right arm.

4. Now notice your left foot. Relax the toes, relax the entire left foot. Relax the ankle. Feel your left leg. Relax the entire left leg. Draw your awareness to the left side of your torso. Relax the left

side of your torso. Relax the left shoulder. Relax the top of the left arm, relax the forearm. Relax the entire left arm.

5. Relax the low back. Relax the middle of your back. Relax the shoulder blades. Relax the neck. Relax the jaw. Relax the tongue. Relax the eyelids. Relax the temples. Relax the brow. Relax the entire head.

Look online for guided body scan meditation if you'd rather have a calming voice lead you through this process.

MEDITATE SIMPLY
BY DOING WHAT YOU LOVE

A wonderful way to get into the present moment is to do things that you love, and to love what you do. If you enjoy swimming, knitting, horseback riding, hiking, reading, singing, dancing, or painting, make time for it in your life. And, as you do the activity, be present and it's a form of meditation!

Leave your stresses and worries behind when you do it, and really enjoy what you're doing. If you're painting, notice the feel of the brush gliding along the paper and how the colorful paint streaks on the page. If you're dancing, let the music pulse through your body. Connect your senses to the activities you choose, and allow yourself to have a good time. Bring this kind of enjoyment to whatever you can in your life. Even in washing the dishes, see if you can appreciate the feel of warm water and sudsy bubbles on your hands. Each time you enjoy a moment rather than dread it, you are cultivating present-moment awareness and contributing positively to your overall well-being.

In your everyday connections, be open about your good feelings about life. Without bragging, and from a genuine place of seeing the good in the moment, tell people what you notice. For those who are interested, eventually, they will also start noticing the good things in life. And this kind of energy resonates in your energy bodies. Their energy and your energy affect the health of the chakras.

TRY AN
OUTDOOR MEDITATION

Nature is the perfect route to meditation and present-moment aware-ness. By stepping outdoors you surround yourself with nature's life force, which is the same energy that runs inside of you. Find activities to do that you would enjoy outside. There is so much variety in nature that you won't get bored even if you take regular walks along the same streets. The sky looks different at sunrise, midday, sunset, mid-night, and the hours in between.

Take a break from your screens on the weekend to go outside and watch cloud formations, find shadows cast by the sun, or stand in the rain and listen to it bounce off your umbrella. At night, look for con-stellations if the sky is clear. When the moon is getting fuller, sit out-side and bathe in the moonlight in the same way you bathe in the sun. Connecting to the life force of nature strengthens the life force in you.

Barefoot Walking

Walking barefoot outside is healthy for you. Breathing fresh air, getting vitamin D from the sunshine, and spending time in water is natural and good. In addition, many believe that standing barefoot on the earth can heal ailments. The intelligent energy of the earth can travel to places in your body that need healing energy.

MEDITATE WHILE
WALKING A LABYRINTH

A labyrinth is constructed as one continuous path that begins at its mouth and curves back and forth according to an ancient pattern, leading to its center. A labyrinth is not a maze, which presents obstacles along the path.

Labyrinths can be used for meditation and spiritual inquiry, which is why they are often found at churches, synagogues, and retreats. As you walk the labyrinth, you feel the supportive earth at your feet and see the expansive sky above your head. The labyrinth truly invites you into a walking meditation. You will find labyrinths of different sizes, in various locations, and constructed with a variety of materials: rocks, tiles, string, clay, plants, lights, paint, and so on. Here are some examples of ways to turn your labyrinth walk into an intentional meditation:

* **Ask a question:** Meditate on a question you feel stuck on and open your heart for guidance. On the way toward the center, ask the universe to release what's keeping you stuck. Once you are in the center, ask the universe for guidance. On the way out, tell the universe that you are open to receiving.
* **Cultivate gratitude:** With each step you take, say "I'm grateful" with sincerity.
* **Walk and meditate:** Focus on taking very slow steps. As thoughts come up, let them go.
* **Honor others:** Hold in your heart loved ones who are living or not and send them your energy.
* **Dance:** Dance or skip along the path.

Or, you can walk the labyrinth with simply an open mind. When you're ready, stand at the beginning of your walk and pause. Walk the labyrinth at whatever pace feels comfortable to you. It's okay to pass others walking the labyrinth if you want to walk faster than they do. Walk the labyrinth to the center. Once in the center, pause and reflect. Stay there as long as you wish. Then follow the path out the same way you came in. After you exit the labyrinth, it is customary to turn toward it and offer gratitude.

Reflect On Your Experience

After walking the labyrinth, you may want to journal or just take some time to think about what you experienced. Often the attitude you bring into the labyrinth mirrors the attitude you bring to the rest of your life. It's a useful mirror in that way. If you walked in a rushed manner, do you notice that you are often rushing in your life? If you are constantly anxious as the labyrinth twists and turns, do you also notice you have a lot of anxiety outside of the labyrinth? If you are completely focused on trying to figure out the path as you walk it, do you find that in your life you have trouble allowing a situation to unfold without it being under your control?

ENJOY A CHAKRA-SPECIFIC
LABYRINTH MEDITATION

You could also meditate on the chakras as you walk the labyrinth. You could do a meditation on each chakra in relation to its element (see Chapter 1). Begin with a visualization of the placement of the Root Chakra and sense your connection to the earth as you enter the labyrinth. After several breaths on the Root Chakra, move your awareness up to the Sacral Chakra, focusing on water. Next, move up to the Solar Plexus Chakra, and so on, arriving at the Crown Chakra when you reach the center.

Another suggestion is to meditate on the chakra in relationship to which loop of the circuit you are on. When you enter a seven-circuit labyrinth pattern, you enter at the third circuit (if you count the walls from the edge, you will see that you enter in three paths from the edge). Then you'll be at the second, first, fourth, seventh, sixth, fifth, and center. You can also meditate on the color or element associated with that chakra. These techniques will bring awareness and energy to the chakras.

MEDITATE
WITH HAIKU

The rules of writing haiku were constructed in the Japanese language, which is very different from the English language. It is customary to hear that haiku must be written in three lines with five syllables in the first and last lines and seven syllables in the second line. However, as time has gone by, people who write haiku in English have tended to think that the number of syllables per line isn't what matters. To write a haiku in English, concentrate more on simply capturing a fleeting moment, evoking a beautiful image of the ephemeral quality of life. You can ignore rules about the number of syllables so that instead you can focus on the thought behind why those rules were made, which was to create simplicity and beauty.

A haiku often captures a moment in nature, and typically includes a word that lets the reader know what season it is. For example, the word daffodils would indicate spring. When you start writing haiku in English usually it's best to use two or three syllables in the first line, five in the second, and three in the last line. Three lines are common. It also helps to read several haiku first, so you can get a sense for how they feel.

Writing and reading haiku are meditative practices and help bring you into the present moment. You can think about certain chakras as you write, or write about topics that are connected to the chakras in some way.

MEDITATE USING THE SO HUM MANTRA
AND YOUR SACRAL CHAKRA

A mantra is a phrase or simple sentence you can think about with intention as you meditate. One of the simplest and most profound mantras is "So Hum"—"I am that I am." Meditating on this simple phrase, you penetrate your layers of protection and self-criticism. As you repeat "So Hum" over and over, you bring your awareness to who you are at the core. The quiet, still place. You discover simply that you exist, that you are.

To do this meditation, sit in a comfortable meditation posture. Feel your sitting bones rooted solidly. Sit up with a steady spine, without trying to straighten out the natural curves. Make sure that the top of your head is parallel to the ceiling, with the back of your neck long. Take a deep inhale in, and let out a long exhale. Take two more deep breaths, making the exhale longer than the inhale. Close your eyes and bring your hands into prayer position at the Heart Chakra. As you breathe in, imagine the syllable "So," and as you breathe out, imagine the syllable "Hum." Do this several times. As you do this, make sure your jaw is relaxed. Begin to feel your entire body relaxing into this mantra.

Place your hands, one on top of the other, at your Sacral Chakra. Inhale deeply, and on the exhale, chant "So Hum." It doesn't matter what musical note you chant. Chant a few times with your hands and attention at your Sacral Chakra, which is the chakra that helps you flow through life and connects you to pleasure. Take pleasure in the simplicity and vastness of this mantra: "I am that I am. So Hum."

The Power of Chants

When you chant or hear chants in Sanskrit, even if you don't know the meaning of the phrases you will receive healing benefits. The vibrations of the syllables produce healing. So chant slowly, listen attentively, and become aware of how the vibration feels. Let it affect you.

USE CHAKRA MEDITATION
TO HELP CHANGE A HABIT

If, after a long day, you always sit in front of the TV or zone out on your phone for several hours, once in a while try something new that helps you check in with your chakras. If your impulse is to watch TV, try going into your meditation space or your room instead. Sit in a comfortable position and follow this chakra meditation practice.

1. Sit in a comfortable position for meditation, with your sitting bones firmly planted on the chair, or on a cushion if you are on the floor. Sit upright, allow the natural curves of the spine to be as they are. Make sure the top of your head is parallel to the ceiling. Gently rest your hands in your lap.
2. After you've read all the following steps, then close your eyes to do them.
3. Relax your jaw, and all the muscles of your face. From top to bottom notice each body part and relax it. Relax the forehead, the jaw, the neck, the shoulders, the arms, the hands, the torso, the belly, the hips, the thighs, the calves, the ankles, and the toes.
4. Breathe naturally for several breaths, and notice the breath as it flows in and as it flows out. Watch and observe how your torso expands on the inhale, and let go on the exhale.
5. Now with your eyes closed, do a chakra scan: at each chakra envision its corresponding color glowing (see Chapter 5). Start at the Crown Chakra. Envision it glowing white, and notice how it and you respond. Relax for several breaths, and notice.
6. Draw your attention down to each chakra, envisioning the color of the chakra for several breaths. Notice how you feel.

7. After you've done this at the Root Chakra, continue to observe the breath for a few moments.

8. Place both of your hands on your body over your heart. Position your hands either in prayer position or with one hand on top of the other facing your heart. Imagine your hands giving your heart energy—loving, restoring energy.

9. When you feel complete, release your hands, and open your eyes.

What you might need at the end of the day is some "me" time, in this way, especially if in your job you have to be "on" or managing others. If you focus a lot of your energy on others, instead of always relaxing in a way that takes you out of yourself (like watching a show or going out for drinks), try coming in to yourself for a change. See how it feels to check in with your chakras. This isn't to suggest you give up *Netflix* or going out altogether. It's about trying something new and seeing if it feels better. You don't have to sacrifice your pleasures altogether to do chakra healing.

EASE A COMMON COLD WITH
A SOLAR PLEXUS MEDITATION

Work on the Solar Plexus Chakra, stoking your internal fire to alleviate a cold.

1. Lie down; cover yourself with blankets to stay warm.
2. Close your eyes, and imagine the glowing sun.
3. Imagine the brightness of the center and the power of its rays. Visualize this for several moments.
4. Inhale deeply, and imagine that you are inhaling the warmth of the sun on a very warm day. Feel the heat enter your nostrils, rise up to your third eye, and then travel down through your energy centers. Exhale toxins. Relax.
5. Again, inhale rays of sun, and when you exhale, release toxins. As you repeat this a few times, imagine your Solar Plexus Chakra beginning to glow brighter and brighter. This is your fiery chakra; ignite it with light and warmth.
6. After you've repeated this breath and visualization, allow your whole body to let go. Relax. And, when you are ready, open your eyes and sit up. Notice how you feel.

Every time you do anything as a healing practice, take time to notice if there's a difference. This brings awareness to the effects, shifting your focus to any improvements and what your body needs next. Are you warmer? Ready for a restorative nap? There is no right or wrong answer; simply notice. If you're thirsty, sip warm water.

MINIMIZE LOW-BACK PAIN
BY FOCUSING ON THE SACRAL CHAKRA

Low-back pain is in the area of the Sacral Chakra. This is the seat of your emotions. When you have low-back pain, slow down and look at what is happening in your emotional realm. Are you angry? Are you concerned about your sex life? Are you emotionally or obsessively attached to someone else? Do you deny or indulge too much in pleasure? Whatever you notice, accept it. Allow it to be there, and then carefully and gingerly find ways to deal with that emotional fire. Grounding practices can help: visualizing the fire moving from the Sacral Chakra through the Root Chakra and into the earth.

Low-back pain can be related to an emotional issue that is deeply rooted, so do more than one practice. You may decide to do chakra healing plus journaling, acupuncture treatment, and dancing in addition to seeking advice and help from other healers and medical doctors.

When emotions get stirred up, energy accumulates and takes up space. It can push organs and other body parts out of their usual place, or at least put pressure on them. Acknowledge the emotions you are having, and give them your attention. Repressing or ignoring them will not help them go away. They will stay buried, causing other illnesses and likely weight gain and retention. Your cells store your memories and emotions. You may notice that sometimes in a yoga class or after exercise you will cry, perhaps without knowing why. In those cases it could be that you dislodged a past feeling or memory, and finally released it. That means you've created more space in your body for prana to flow, which brings overall health.

CHAPTER 9

BALANCING CHAKRAS WITH AROMATHERAPY

One of the fastest ways to create and notice a change in your energy field is to use aromatherapy. Aromatherapy is a healing modality that uses natural essential oils to heal the body, mind, and spirit. The aromas from essential oils can promote relaxation, clear thinking, positive outlook, and greater health. There are a variety of ways to experience aromatherapy. You can use quick-and-easy methods to feel more relaxed, or you can create longer and more luxurious experiences. Whichever you choose, as you inhale the aromas your body will begin to respond, and if you surrender you will notice a change in your mental, physical, and energetic bodies.

The essential oils used in aromatherapy are highly potent, concentrated oils from trees, plants, and grasses. The scents, energy, and properties of the oils can heal and protect you from illness, disease, and imbalance. There are many different essential oils and ways they can be used, so it's best to have training, buy a comprehensive guide on aromatherapy, and/or talk to someone who is well trained for sound advice about which oils to use for the results you desire.

Not everyone agrees on which essential oils support each chakra. Each person is slightly different, and responses will vary. Seek advice from someone who is experienced and well-informed and combine that information with your own experience of how the essential oils affect you. Their knowledge combined with your personal experience is the best indicator for which essential oils you will favor for balance.

ENJOY AN
AROMATHERAPY MASSAGE

A trained professional gives aromatherapy massage by selecting the appropriate oils to mix in a base carrier oil. The essential oils are highly potent and so are not meant to be applied directly to the skin. A base carrier oil is a pure oil, such as extra-virgin cold-pressed olive oil or sesame oil, that can be used to dilute essential oils.

If you would like to do self-massage with essential oils, get the best carrier oil that you can from a specialist store. What you put on your body gets absorbed into your body, so you want only the purest and best oil when you apply it to your skin. Then add drops of the essential oil to the base carrier. A typical recipe is to measure the amount of base oil in milliliters, and then divide that number in half to give you the maximum number of drops of essential oil that you will need.

After testing the oil on the skin to make sure there is no allergic reaction (see box), you can do a healing self-massage. First put a couple of drops of the mixture of base oil and essential oil onto your hands and rub your hands together to stimulate the scent of the oil. Bring the palms of your hands up to your face, and inhale the scent for several breaths. Then gently begin to massage the top of your head, at the crown. Then slowly progress down the body, giving your body the attention it deserves. Continue to inhale the aroma that gently wafts through the air.

When you've finished with the massage, relax. Allow the effects of the massage to sink in. Envision the healing occurring; enjoy the process.

Before You Use Essential Oils

Test the mixture of essential oils and base carrier on the skin of the receiver by first applying a small amount to the inside of the wrist, then behind the knee, and/or in the crease of the elbow. Check the spot twenty-four hours later to see if the skin had a reaction or not.

CLEAR DISTURBANCES
WITH AN ENERGETIC MASSAGE

You can also do an aromatherapy energetic self-massage without touching your body. For the energetic massage, mix the essential oils with a high-quality base carrier oil, as directed in Enjoy an Aromatherapy Massage. Place a few drops of the elixir into your hands. Rub your hands together to release the scent of the oils. Bring the palms of your hands to your face to inhale the scent for several breaths and call to mind the healing properties of the oils. Inhale and exhale several times. Then hold your hands about 6 to 10 inches from your body and do an energetic sweep of your entire body. Slowly sweep downward, brushing away unwanted disturbance in the energy field.

After you've completed this, relax for several moments. Notice the effects. Then wash your hands with cold water.

Healing Power of Lavender

Historically, lavender has been used as an antiseptic and for mental health support. Today, it's used for its sedative and calming qualities. Lavender is used to treat anxiety, insomnia, and depression. It can also be used to alleviate headaches and upset stomach.

DIFFUSE
ESSENTIAL OILS

Instead of applying a mixture of base carrier oil and essential oils to the skin, you can receive the healing benefits of essential oils by diffusing them into the air. There are specific diffusers made to use with essential oils. (Read the directions because each diffuser works differently.) Diffusers have a humidifying benefit to combat the dryness in the air, and they also help sanitize and infuse the air with healing properties. For example, you can diffuse lavender in the air to promote relaxation and serenity, or tea tree oil for its antiviral and antibacterial properties.

STEAM OR BATHE
WITH ESSENTIAL OILS

When the air is dry, steaming with an essential oil is a simple, fast, and effective way to receive therapeutic benefits. The vapor infused with healing properties rises into the nasal passages, entering your system immediately.

1. Have a towel and your essential oil nearby.
2. Get a bowl that is approximately 10 to 12 inches in diameter.
3. Boil enough water to fill the bowl one-half to two-thirds full.
4. Pour the steaming water into the bowl, and then add one drop of the essential oil to the bowl.
5. Lean your head into the flow of the steam, and put the towel over your head to cover your head and the bowl.
6. Inhale deeply through both nostrils, exhale gently through the mouth. Repeat this several times.
7. If you would like to, also close one nostril with your finger, and inhale and exhale through one nostril at a time to make sure that each side is receiving the benefits.
8. If one drop of the essential oil wasn't strong enough, or if the scent diminishes, add another drop. It's doubtful you will need more than two drops of the essential oil.
9. When you are finished steaming, sit down. Take a moment to notice the effects. Practice this two to three times per day if you're working with a particular imbalance or onset of a cold.

Another way to enjoy steaming with an essential oil is to use the elixir in the bath. First dilute the essential oil in a base carrier oil, then pour ¼ cup of the mixture into your bath. The oil will be absorbed through your skin, and inhaled through your nostrils. This is a soothing, relaxing, and natural way to feel healthy.

CHOOSE OILS FOR
SPECIFIC CHAKRAS

Particular essential oils are said to balance specific chakras. When you inhale the scents of the aromas, you can also practice visualizations. Visualize the healing energy traveling to the parts of your body that need it most. With every inhale, envision the healing mist entering your body, and with every exhale release the toxins. Here are specific oils that can help specific chakras:

* **Root:** As your connection to the earth, when the Root Chakra is balanced you will feel grounded. To balance this chakra you may choose essential oils from a plant that has earthy and red-toned colors. Suggested oils are patchouli, myrrh, and cedarwood.
* **Sacral:** The Sacral Chakra is associated with fluidity, creation, sexuality, and emotions. You want essential oils that will calm the emotions and ease fear of change. Recommended essential oils are sandalwood, jasmine, and rose.
* **Solar Plexus:** The Solar Plexus Chakra is also a fiery energy center. While the Sacral Chakra can be fiery with unbalanced emotions and sexuality, too much fire in the Solar Plexus Chakra is associated with becoming judgmental, controlling, and angry. So, again, you will want scents that calm down fire: cooling, flowery, calming scents.
* **Heart:** The Heart Chakra is such a powerful transmitter for love, compassion, and maintaining authentic relationship. When it's out of balance, not only will you feel unsatisfied in your relationships, you also will have diminished perceptive abilities. This could lead to more misunderstandings and miscommunications, and fuel the pain of an imbalanced Heart Chakra because of cloudy perception. Essential oils recommended for the Heart

Chakra are rose, lemon balm (*Melissa officinalis*), and neroli (bitter orange). Also, tree scents such as pine and cedar can be beneficial because the Heart Chakra responds to green, and the cedar and pine trees are green in their natural form.

* **Throat:** Chamomile and thyme are two herbs recommended for an imbalance in the Throat Chakra. If you notice you are constantly talking, monopolizing the conversation time you share with others, and feeling needy for conversation, you may have an overactive Throat Chakra. If you are withholding your opinion and voice, you may have an underactive Throat Chakra. In either of these cases, using chamomile or thyme could help. Lavender is also an option. It's an all-around useful oil, and notice that it's a color that can be associated with this and the Third Eye Chakra.

* **Third Eye:** The Third Eye Chakra is enhanced by frankincense, basil, and rose geranium. Frankincense promotes deep relaxation and breath awareness. It helps you access dream states, past lives, and deep meditative states. Basil helps with clear thinking, and helps to decrease stress and nervousness. Both frankincense and basil help with congestion and respiratory infections.

* **Crown:** The Crown Chakra, like the third eye, is a prime location for putting any of the essential oils because of the proximity to the brain. The essential oils that are recommended for this chakra are ylang-ylang and rosewood. Both these scents are said to connect you to the universal energy, helping you to experience out-of-this-world states of relaxation and bliss.

CHAPTER 10

BALANCING CHAKRAS TO MANIFEST YOUR DESIRES

Your thoughts become your reality. Being intentional about your thoughts, words, and actions is how you create your life's path, moment by moment. The Law of Attraction explains that your thoughts and desires are vibrations that emanate from you out into the universe. In response, the universe begins to answer your requests. Like attracts like: as you have thoughts, more related thoughts come to you and bolster your thoughts/desires. The universe conspires to make it so, as you continue to give strength to the original thought. Both chakra healing and the Law of Attraction explain that when universal energy flows through you in a balanced way, you experience overall health and the life your heart desires. Taking time in your life to practice chakra healing and getting used to keeping in mind the Law of Attraction is a perfect combination to create the conditions to allow the natural flow of energy. The exercises in this chapter will help you use chakra healing and the Law of Attraction to achieve your goals and live your best life.

EXIST IN HARMONY
WITH THE UNIVERSE

The Law of Attraction is not activated based on whether or not you believe in it. The Law of Attraction is working right now, everywhere, all the time. As you begin to learn about it you will begin to understand how to lead the life you want to lead, how to attract circumstances you desire, and how to create fewer obstacles for yourself in the process. You'll do that by being in sync with yourself and the universe around you.

After all, you are not separate from the earth. With every inhale and exhale you are plugging in to the same energy that sustains the entire universe. The healthy food you eat and the water you drink come from nature. You receive your energy and physical sustenance from the earth, which means your vibrations and needs are compatible with the vibrations and gifts of the earth. The fuel of the earth is fuel for your physical body. You thrive when you exist in harmony with nature.

Your body, when in a state of energetic balance, can perform all its functions to keep you healthy. If you can believe that the universe and you are both interested in well-being, you can begin to live from a place of belief that harmony is the natural state of things. The world is not out to get you, trick you, or make your life difficult. In fact, the universe provides you with all you need for health, joy, and fulfillment.

Just as your physical body is compatible with earth's produce, on an energetic level your vibrations are compatible with the other vibrations in the universe. This includes the vibrations of plants, animals, and water. Your vibrations resonate outward into the universe and the universe answers your request. According to the Law of Attraction, the universe works to match the vibrations you send out, bringing your desires into being as soon as seven seconds after you feel the desire. Your task, after putting your desires out there, is to be receptive.

GET CLEAR ABOUT
WHAT YOU WANT

If you don't already know what you most desire, spend time getting to know what your heart's desire is. If you don't spend time on self-inquiry and self-care, consider whether you might instead be spending too much of your energy focused on others. Focusing on others can come in the form of replaying over and over what someone has said to you, putting lots of interest in what others are doing (or not doing), dwelling on what's not right with you or the world, and wishing other people would change. Caring about others and their well-being is compassionate and beneficial. It can be a slippery slope, though. If you are focusing so much on others that you do not attend to what you need and can create in your life, then focusing on others could be an escape. Cultivate the balance between giving to others and nourishing your health and dreams.

The beauty of manifesting your desires is that you don't have to struggle to attract what you want. You have to know what you want and then enjoy the process. Enjoyment is an important part of the manifestation process. The effort is the part where you strip away the chatter and the noise to find out what you really want in your life. You examine where you are, what you are grateful for, and what you would like to attract. In this process, it's important to be very specific. There's no need to feel guilty or embarrassed about what you want. Make the list detailed. Whether it's a list of the qualities you want in a partner or a detailed description of a house you would like to buy, go for it! The more specific you are, the more likely it is that you will get exactly what you want.

As you make this effort, you don't need to struggle. Make this easeful. You are creating what you want in your life. Doesn't that sound good? Enjoy the process.

BE READY TO RECEIVE
WHAT YOU ASKED FOR

After you've asked for what you desire and you've become patient to allow the universe to do its part, the last step is receiving it. This step can sometimes be thwarted because if you have given up too soon, and/or if you have focused your attention elsewhere or on the "lack" of it, then you won't be in the place to receive what you asked for. While your life is unfolding, and you know what you've asked for, the Law of Attraction is supported by your joyful expectation.

With each new creation that you manifest, you will experience change in your life. If you've asked for a new partner, a new house, a new career, more money, etc., inevitably the new circumstances will create change. Sometimes people resist change, however. Even if something "good" comes their way, they may not be ready to take it and make the change they thought they wanted.

When what you asked for comes into your life, trust that you can handle the newness, the unknown. In the time it's taken the desire to manifest, you've grown and changed with the thoughts you've had about this new idea. Know that with each new step comes the invitation for yet another one. You are constantly changing, life is constantly changing, and you play a part in how it unfolds. Change can bring about delightful experiences.

Appreciate What You Have

Appreciation is one of the most wonderful feelings to experience. Once you receive what you've asked for, take time to appreciate it. Appreciating is pausing to notice the beauty and support that you have in the universe.

CULTIVATE FEARLESSNESS
WITH YOUR CROWN CHAKRA

According to the Law of Attraction if you have resistant thoughts to what you desire, you are blocking what you want from coming to you. For example, if you want a new house, and also you are afraid that you can't perform all of the upkeep, worried about moving all of your things into a new home, and concerned that you won't like the new house as much as your present home, then you are sending out the signals that you don't really want a new house. See if your fears are really telling you something important, and if not, see if you can shift your attitude to contentment around the new house. This will allow the positive outcome to flow to you.

To use chakra healing and the Law of Attraction to help cultivate fearlessness, buy a clear quartz or amethyst crystal that you can hold in the palms of your hands. It will support your Crown Chakra for this exercise.

1. Have the crystal nearby, but not yet in your hands.
2. Take a moment to bring to mind one big thing that your heart desires. Allow your mind to go to what fears you may have around receiving this next thing. If you want, write the fears down now. Then place the paper to the side.
3. Pick up the crystal, and hold it inside your cupped hands: one hand on top of the other, with the crystal inside.
4. Feel the energy of the crystal in your hands. Feel the energy travel through your arms, into your entire body, cleansing your body of doubt, fear, or anxiety. If you don't feel it, it's okay. Visualize it.

5. Breathe in and out naturally for several breaths while envisioning the pure, vibrant energy replacing insecurities held in your body and mind.
6. Put the crystal down, and on a new piece of paper write down how you are feeling now. Notice if there have been any positive shifts in your energy.
7. Throw away or safely burn the piece of paper with your fears on it.

Notice if you feel more relaxed after these several moments of breathing and visualizing new energy pulsing through your body. Feel a connection to love, and from this place, think about your choices. Envision how you want things to be, and fill that vision with your pure, positive intentions.

PRACTICE THE ART OF LETTING GO
BY FOCUSING ON YOUR SOLAR PLEXUS

Once you have cultivated a clear vision of what you are attracting into your life, relax around it. Let it go. Give it time to manifest. When what you want comes to mind, feed it with positive thoughts, take the appropriate actions to bring it into being, but don't cling to it. Don't worry that you have to push, push, push to get what you want. Give it space.

When you want to let go and allow things to take their course, strengthening any and all of the chakras always helps. Specifically, if you are feeling insecure, try this exercise to balance the Solar Plexus Chakra:

1. Sit in a position for meditation.
2. Place your hands one on top of the other on your solar plexus.
3. Practice Kapalabhati breath (see Chapter 7). If you are new to it, just practice ten exhales. If you are used to it, do thirty. Relax, then repeat two more times.
4. Notice how you feel.
5. Keeping your hands where they are, and while breathing normally, envision glowing yellow light emanating from your hands into your third chakra. Do this for several moments.
6. When you are done with this visualization, take a moment to come back to the present moment.

This visualization and Kapalabhati exercise is meant to strengthen your Solar Plexus Chakra. Do not perform Kapalabhati if you have uncontrolled high blood pressure, if you are pregnant, if you have recently had surgery, if you are menstruating, if you have stomach or digestive trouble, or if you have high anxiety. If you have these conditions, try Nadi Shodhana (see Chapter 7) for fifteen minutes each morning and/or evening. And do the visualization included in steps 5 and 6 of this exercise for balancing the Solar Plexus Chakra.

KEEP AN OPEN HEART
BY WISHING OTHERS WELL

As you are practicing enjoying the moment now and also manifesting things for the future, keep an open heart. This is not as easy as it sounds. The heart is very perceptive, and as such it will close down to protect itself. If you are expending too much attention outward or if you are being overloaded with too much needy attention, the heart will become blocked. You can open your heart when it will serve you by focusing on your Heart Chakra.

Send loving thoughts from your Heart Chakra to your friends and loved ones to help keep your heart open. You can also hold a specific person in your mind's eye, and send him or her a powerful wish: "May you be happy. May you be healthy. May you know peace." When you are truly able to wish everyone peace and happiness, even those with whom you feel conflict, you will know your heart is open. When you balance your Heart Chakra, you are connected to the feeling of oneness of all that is. That's the space to be in as you manifest your own desires.

STRENGTHEN YOUR THROAT CHAKRA
BY JOURNALING YOUR INTENTIONS

Journaling is a great way to strengthen your Throat Chakra, which is about expressing yourself in the world. As you express yourself in writing, you are practicing hearing and seeing your own voice. What thoughts do you have toward your own voice? What thoughts do you have about your own writing? Do the thoughts about your writing mirror thoughts you have about yourself in general? Notice which chakras match up to the feelings you are having. Then balance blocked chakras. Always, in addition to any chakras you strengthen through journaling, the act of journaling itself strengthens your Throat Chakra. You might choose to write down your intentions and the desires you wish to manifest.

If you want to bring healing to a particular chakra, write how you experience the physical and psychological issues of that chakra. If your experience indicates a blocked chakra, write "What emotions are associated with this imbalance?" Then put pen to paper and see what answer you write. Once you find out what emotions are involved, you'll know which chakra to heal.

Often, journaling allows you to discover what answers will come. You can journal for self-discovery and to reveal your own inner wisdom that you don't always access throughout your day. If you allow the thoughts to flow with patience and an open heart, you will find the answers that you seek. The more you find answers to who you are, what you need, and what you desire, the more intentional you can be about placing your energy on what you want to manifest in your life.

CONDUCT A MORNING CHAKRA CHECK-IN AND INTENTION-SETTING RITUAL

Adding a chakra check-in and intention-setting period to your morning is a great way to be mindful of how you want to feel during your day. After you have washed your face and brushed your teeth, take a moment to see how you are feeling, and set an intention.

The intention you set can come from what you notice in the moment about your chakras. For example, if you feel that your heart is heavy this morning, set an intention such as, "Today my heart is well, open, and strong," and visualize sending green energy to your heart space. Use that as your mantra for the day. Write your intention on a piece of paper and bring it with you. You can put it in your pocket, tape it to the back of your phone, or tape it to the dashboard of your car. If you put it somewhere where you'll see it, then you'll have an easier time remembering it throughout your day.

If you are feeling ungrounded and separate from your body, sit on the floor and notice that you are held up by the earth. Or stand tall and feel your feet firmly connected to the earth. Then say to yourself "All day I am safe, stable, and connected." Feel the support of the earth underneath you.

Repeat the intention three times, with your eyes closed, envisioning it to be true. As you envision it as true, you are creating that reality. If you think you'll be anxious all day, then it would be hard for you to feel otherwise. When you notice an imbalance in your psychology or physical body in the morning, ask yourself which chakra that connects to, then set your intention in a way that supports that chakra's function.

RECITE AFFIRMATIONS
FOR CHAKRA HEALING

When visualizing the future, it's important to continue to give yourself positive affirmations that emphasize your inherent power and abilities. All affirmations are good and healing for your chakras. The following table offers simple affirmations you can attach to each chakra, based on the psychological issues associated with each.

Chakra Healing Affirmations	
Affirmation	**Chakra**
I am safe, I am supported	Root
I feel, I flow	Sacral
I act, I can	Solar Plexus
I love, I receive love	Heart
I speak, I listen	Throat
I see	Third Eye
I am	Crown

When you do chakra healing affirmations, you strengthen each chakra with the vibration that supports its proper functioning. You can envision colors while you do this, you can hold appropriate crystals to bolster the healing energy, or you could simply do the affirmations and be with what comes up. All of these ways are valuable and effective methods for bringing energy to the chakras It's amazing how helpful self-affirmation is. The messages you tell yourself directly affect your overall health and the life you create.

GLOSSARY

Adrenals:
Part of the endocrine system. They support your body in stressful situations, activating your fight-or-flight response. The adrenals attach to the kidneys.

Ajna:
The Third Eye or Brow Chakra. It means "to perceive." The chakra is located between the eyes and slightly above the brow line. The Ajna Chakra is said to radiate an indigo glow.

Allopathic medicine:
Uses surgery and drugs to combat disease, also considered conventional medicine.

Alternative healing practices:
Healing modalities that are not considered conventional practices by Western medical standards. Alternative practices include, but are not limited to, mind-body medicine, natural remedies, energy work, and bodywork. These practices are considered alternative when used instead of allopathic treatments.

Anahata:
The Heart Chakra. The name means "unstruck," and the chakra is said to have a green glow.

Aromatherapy:
The use of the scents of essential oils to soothe and heal body, mind, and spirit.

Asana:
Any of the physical postures of Hatha yoga practice.

Aura:
The energetic field surrounding the body. It can be seen by the naked eye and in kirlian photography.

Chakra:
Sanskrit for "wheel or disc." Spinning vortices of energy.

Complementary healing practices:
Healing modalities that are used in conjunction with allopathic medicine to support the healing process. Complementary modalities include, but are not limited to, mind-body medicine, natural remedies, energy work, and bodywork.

Essential oils:
Potent oils distilled from flowers, plants, trees, and grasses that are used in aromatherapy to promote and sustain wellness.

Hatha yoga:
The physical practice of yoga postures.

Ida nadi:
One of the three major energy channels in the body. The ida nadi starts at the Third Eye Chakra and first curves to the left before crossing the sushumna at the Throat Chakra, then curving to the right. It

crisscrosses with the pingala nadi back and forth all the way down to the Root Chakra.

Islets of Langerhans:
Part of the endocrine system, located in the pancreas. They are responsible for the secretion of insulin.

Kirlian photograph:
A photograph that captures an aura as visible light.

Kirtan:
Call-and-response chanting, usually of mantras from the Indian spiritual traditions.

Koshas:
The five sheaths or layers that are the physical, energetic, mental, knowing, and spiritual parts of the body.

Kundalini:
The serpent goddess who is said to be coiled around the Root Chakra, until she is awakened and travels up the seven chakras to unite with divine consciousness at the Crown Chakra.

Lumbar vertebrae:
The lower part of the spine above the sacrum, consisting of five vertebrae.

Manipura:
Referred to as "lustrous gem," the Solar Plexus Chakra is said to glow a bright yellow.

Meridians:
Energy channels in the body mapped out in Chinese medicine, especially useful for acupuncture, acupressure, and reflexology.

Muladhara:
The Root Chakra, said to glow a deep red.

Nadi:
Energy channel in the body.

Nirvana:
State of liberation from the physical body.

Niyama:
Special observances for how to take care of your mind, body, and spirit on the eight-limbed path of yoga.

Om:
The universal sound; the primordial sound; the sound of God, energy, and spirit.

Parasympathetic nervous system:
Creates the relaxation response.

Pericarp:
The fleshy part of the fruit or flower that protects the seed.

Perineum:
The area of the body between the genitals and the anus.

Pineal gland:
Part of the endocrine system that secretes serotonin and melanin.

Pingala nadi:
One of the three major energy channels in the body. The pingala nadi starts at the Third Eye Chakra and first curves to the right before crossing the sushumna at the Throat Chakra, then curving to the left. It crisscrosses with the ida nadi back and forth all the way down to the Root Chakra.

Pituitary:
A gland of the endocrine system that influences growth, metabolism, and many chemical processes in the body.

Prana:
Life-force energy.

Pranayama:
Breath and energy control.

Sahasrara:
Literally means "thousandfold," it's the Crown Chakra, and glows white, gold, or purple.

Sushumna:
The central energy channel of the body that is located in the spine.

Svadhisthana:
Meaning "sweetness," this is the Sacral Chakra, said to glow a bright orange.

Sympathetic nervous system:
Activated when you are in fight-or-flight response, increases your heart rate and prepares you for action.

Theosophist:
A student of theosophy.

Theosophy:
A school of mystical thought founded in 1875, inspired by yogic philosophy.

Thymus:
A gland in the endocrine system responsible for supporting your immune system.

Thyroid:
A gland in the endocrine system that supports metabolism.

Upanishads:
Vedic philosophy.

Visuddha:
The Throat Chakra. In Sanskrit it means "purification." It is said to have a blue glow.

Whole systems of health:
Medical practices that are comprehensive in theory and practice, and separate from conventional Western medicine. These include Ayurveda, Chinese medicine, and homeopathy.

INDEX